Celebrating Strengths

Building Strengths-based Schools

Jennifer M. Fox Eades
Foreword by Anthony Seldon

CAPP Press
Coventry, England

Other Books in the CAPP Press *Strengthening the World series*

Average to A+: Realising Strengths in Yourself and Others
Alex Linley

Other Books by Jennifer Fox Eades

Classroom Tales: Using Story Telling to Build Emotional, Social and Academic Skills Across the Primary Curriculum
Published 2005 by Jessica Kingsley, London

Listening to Life: A Practical Approach to Spiritual and Emotional Development in the Classroom
Published 2004 by Cromwell Press, Trowbridge

In memory of

Charles Robert Fox

1924-1966

Deputy Head Teacher

Barlby Primary School, Ladbroke Grove, London

Teachers change the world every day through acts of kindness, courage, hope and integrity. This book is dedicated to my father, a teacher who changed lives for the better and who inspires me to try to do the same.

CAPP PRESS

The Venture Centre
University of Warwick Science Park
Coventry CV4 7EZ
United Kingdom
Tel: +44 (0)24 76 323 363
Fax: +44 (0)24 76 323 001
Email: capp@cappeu.org
Website: www.capp-press.org

CAPP Press is a trading name of the Centre for Applied Positive Psychology, a
not-for-profit company limited by guarantee, registered in England and Wales,
company number 05589865

First published in the United Kingdom in 2008

© CAPP Press 2008

ISBN: 978-1-906366-01-8 (hardback)
ISBN: 978-1-906366-02-5 (paperback)

British Library Cataloguing-in-Publication Data
A catalogue record for this book is available from the British Library.

Typesetting and design by Book Production Services, London

Printed in the United Kingdom

10 9 8 7 6 5 4 3 2 1

It is the policy of CAPP Press to use paper from sources that are SFI
(Sustainable Forestry Initiative) and PEFC (Programme for the Endorsement
of Forest Certification Schemes) Certified.

CONTENTS

SERIES EDITOR'S FOREWORD   VII

FOREWORD   IX

PREFACE   II

Part One - Three Threads

1 Introduction   3
2 Positive Psychology in Education   19
3 Strengths and Strengths Gym   34
4 Stories and Story Telling   46
5 Festivals and Celebration   64

Part Two - Three Levels

6 Celebrating Strengths in the Individual   83
7 Celebrating Strengths in the Classroom   97
8 Celebrating Strengths in the Wider School 114

Part Three - The Festivals

 9 Beginnings   127
10 Thanksgiving, Harvest, Sukkot or Raksha Bandhan   145

11 Festivals of Light: Advent, Divali, Hannukah, Eid   159

12 Performing Arts   172

13 Easter: A Celebration of Love, Kindness and Friendship   190

14 Our Community   201

15 Endings   212

16 Creating Your Own Festivals   226

17 In Conclusion: Where to Begin?   233

NOTES   235

APPENDIX: Sources for stories   242

INDEX   244

SERIES EDITOR'S FOREWORD

I FIRST HEARD about Jenny Fox Eades' amazing work in schools through a colleague in the United States. Despite the fact that Jenny and I are based less than two hundred miles from each other, it still took someone four thousand miles away to connect us. "Take a look at this amazing work being done in schools using strengths and positive psychology," I was told. I am familiar with the grand claims that are often made for things, and even more familiar with the regularity with which the reality fails to live up to these grand claims. In Jenny's case, this was quite the opposite: the impact and importance of her work were understated, and the more I learn about them, the more I realise how understated they were.

This book tells the story of how Jenny has taken some of the best ideas to come out of psychology in the last fifty years, and translated them into practical applications that children and teachers can use in their classrooms and in their schools. The book is about celebrating all of the strengths that exist in a school – in children, teachers and other staff. It is about using that celebration to enhance the environment and the experience for all who are involved with it. We should all be indebted to Jenny for providing a resource that will be of lasting impact and importance, while keeping the material so accessible and useful - not only to practitioners in education, but to any adult involved in children's lives.

The *Strengthening the World* series from CAPP Press publishes books that enable people to understand and realise more of their strengths, and to create the settings and environments that support them in doing so. We are honoured that Jenny chose to work with the CAPP Press on this project, and I am delighted to include this volume as one of the first books in our *Strengthening the World* series.

Alex Linley
Series Editor
CAPP Press *Strengthening the World* Series

Foreword

THE MOST IMPORTANT development in the content of British schools so far this century has been the application of positive psychology. The last few years has seen the dawning realisation that it has a vital role to play in enhancing the lives of children and teachers. Positive psychology is an import from the United States, developed by Professor Martin Seligman of the University of Pennsylvania and drawing from the work of Daniel Goleman and others on emotional intelligence. Its central insight is that lessons can be learnt from psychology about how individuals and organisations can flourish. Traditional psychology was concerned with understanding and coping with mental and institutional abnormality. This was all very well, but offered schools little for the majority. Positive psychology, properly understood and applied, offers insights for every child and every adult within the schools.

The assumption that schools had no responsibility for developing the emotional well-being of its children has begun to break down in the last few years. It is increasingly accepted that, if children are to reach their full potential, schools cannot merely teach traditional subjects with a bit of PSHE, sport and culture thrown in. They need to do much more to develop in their children resilience, powers of self-restraint and the habits of optimistic thinking. Allied to this new thinking has been a far more systematic approach to the teaching of mental and physical well-being, with schools realising that they shoulder a major responsibility for developing wholeness in each child. The British government of Gordon Brown since June 2007 has adopted an encouraging attitude to the development of emotional intelligence, and is extending its existing programme from primary to secondary schools. But many others in politics, as well as in education and the media, are still highly sceptical about whether "well-being" can or should be taught to the young. They have no answer to the question that "If it is not taught at schools, and it is not adequately covered at home, when will it be?"

Into this debate comes this very important book by Jenny Fox Eades. Her experience as an independent education advisor helping to introduce positive psychology in areas of social deprivation has equipped her very well in the writing of this book. She has a very clear understanding of the complex literature written by academic psychologists, and translates it into a book that teachers will want to read. Her secret is not only her clear prose, but also the way that she makes her book so practical. Her direct experience of schools helps her to see the world through the eyes of the teacher. The book is full of hands on wisdom and suggestions as to how teachers can adapt the wisdom of positive psychology for themselves and in the classroom.

Positive, centred teachers are far more willing and able to create the right atmosphere for real learning to take place. The current absurdity in Britain of over-testing, over-examining and fear-inducing inspection leads to stress and is wholly un-conducive to the development of an intelligent school in the fullest sense.

It is the development of an intelligent school which is the core objective of Jenny Fox Eades' remarkable *Celebrating Strengths*. I would encourage every teacher, every parent and all concerned with education to read and practise it.

Anthony Seldon
Wellington College

CELEBRATING STRENGTHS IS about building strengths-based schools. Its aim is to help teachers identify and use more of their own strengths and then to provide ideas for helping pupils do the same.

Celebrating Strengths takes ancient wisdom and links it to modern scientific insights to produce lasting, positive change. The result is a unique and powerful method of introducing and sustaining positive lasting change in schools. Its primary goal is to support teachers because teachers deserve support. Theirs is one of the hardest and most valuable jobs in the world – to inspire a new generation with a love of learning. I want teachers to flourish and enjoy their work because it is only when teachers flourish that children can flourish too.

Its subsidiary goals are to enhance pupil and teacher enjoyment of schools and education, to help children develop a life long love of learning and to become healthy, resilient, positive adults. And it works! We know that because we have been using it in a cluster of schools in Scunthorpe for nearly four years. All of the schools have used Celebrating Strengths in their own unique way to develop and build on their existing strengths and to become truly strengths-based schools. Teachers have grown in confidence, pupils have gained in maturity and self esteem. Your school can do the same. Celebrating Strengths is meant to be enjoyable, it is meant to be adaptable, it is meant to be done a little at a time or all at once if you prefer. Small changes add up – introduce one idea, tell one story and you will make a positive difference. We change the world one small step at a time – but we change it! That's our job as teachers. This book is intended to help.

I owe enormous thanks to Daryl Summers who gave me the opportunity to develop this work in Scunthorpe and to the staff and children of Riddings Infant school. Also to Ewart Gibbs and Alison Laidlaw and all the staff at Leys Farm who helped me to see the potential of strengths based work at key stage 2. Thanks also to John Bonham and the staff and children of Riddings Junior School and to Caroline Raby and the staff and children of Enderby Road Infant School.

A very special thank you to Diane Barratt, who first invited me to work at Riddings Infants and with whom I designed all the festivals described here. Diane has the courage to take risks – and achieves excellence as a result. Thank you Diane.

The book is divided into three sections. Part One describes some of the theory and ideas that underpin *Celebrating Strengths*. Part Two describes how these can be put into practice for individuals, in the classroom and in the school as a whole. Part Three includes outlines of seven festivals you might celebrate, with ideas for stories and activities (called Strengths Builders), making them memorable and celebrating strengths all the year round. You can take the chapters and use them as a basis for a festival, or you can adapt them to suit yourself. Whether you read the book right through, or dip in and out of it according to your interest, I hope you enjoy it. And most importantly of all, I hope it adds value and vitality to your life and those of the children around you.

Jenny Fox Eades
Cheshire, July 2007

PART ONE

Three Threads

ONE

Introduction

TEACHERS ARE IMPORTANT people – they change lives. Schools are important places – they are where children experience a community dedicated to learning in its broadest sense. A single good teacher who cares and shows that they care, who is passionate about children, about learning and about life, can inspire a child and have an influence beyond their own life span. I know this for a fact because my father was such a teacher. This book is dedicated to him. However, I know little about him because he died when I was only three. Recently it occurred to me that I might find memories of him from people he taught on the website Friends Reunited. So I went looking and I did indeed find memories – inspiring memories. 'Due to your father I played football and cricket for the school. He was a lovely man and he was really my mentor because he had confidence in my abilities. I can picture him now, watching me play in goal during the break periods from the top floor window.' Now the man who wrote those words runs his own business, following his passions and doing work that he loves, while his five sons work with him.

My father changed the world, just a little, by small acts of kindness and integrity and hope, and his influence has outlived him by many years. I know that the vast majority of teachers do the same and Celebrating Strengths is intended to help and support them in doing that. It celebrates the teacher's strengths first and then gives practical ideas for helping them to emphasise and build on the strengths of the pupils they work with. Little changes, little acts of kindness and integrity and hope add up – and eventually change the world.

Celebrating Strengths is a tried and tested tool for building and maintaining a strengths-based school. It has been used and refined by teachers and children. It develops well-being and resilience, helps build strong communities, increases confidence and produces positive change that is deep seated and long lasting by combining the latest psychological research with ancient insights and teaching methods. It began life as a three year pilot project in four infant and junior schools in Scunthorpe and developed with the help of the creativity, courage and enthusiasm of the staff and pupils of each of those communities.

Celebrating Strengths is a tool that uses practical methods – methods like oral story telling, celebrating festivals, noticing and building on strengths. You may be using such methods already – they are not new. What Celebrating Strengths does is to draw on the latest research from positive psychology and children's mental health to show **why** such methods are important. Celebrating Strengths, by linking and combining areas that were previously treated as separate, makes these areas even more effective. Celebrating Strengths builds on your own individual strengths and those of your school and gives you ideas for how to use them even more effectively.

Celebrating Strengths is not a blueprint. I do not feel that hard working teachers need to be told what to do and how to do it yet again. Rather, it is meant to inspire you to use your own creativity, to give hints, suggestions, ideas for you to use, change, adapt or do the opposite of, to suit yourself and your pupils and your school.

Small changes add up. Adopt one small positive change and you will have made a difference – adopts lots of changes and you will make that difference even greater - but remember, you can still do that one step at a time.

The goal of Celebrating Strengths is to build flourishing school communities, flourishing staff, flourishing pupils. Bored teachers and bored children do not sparkle and do not reach their potential. Celebrating Strengths is meant to be enjoyable and supportive. It incorporates approaches that will refresh and support the adults in the community as well as the children – because stressed, harassed teachers are not good for children and are not good for themselves either.

Celebrating Strengths is intended to foster a love of learning and build strength of character. We have had so much anxiety about targets and attainment in recent years that it has become hard to keep a firm grasp of what education is actually supposed to be about – inspiring children with a love of learning that will last a life time and helping them to develop into thoughtful, caring, ethical individuals who will make a positive difference to the world. Celebrating Strengths draws on findings from positive psychology and child mental health to help children to become resilient and optimistic individuals, but it incorporates these insights into the curriculum rather than offering yet another subject for teachers to teach. The curriculum is too crowded already. What is needed is more time for reflection – not more content. Celebrating Strengths offers strategies for building reflection into the school day.

Forming Positive Habits

Celebrating Strengths uses specific methods to build flourishing communities. One of the main methods is the formation of positive habits. Lasting change happens when a change becomes a habit. If you make a change – in your diet or exercise regime for example – and it requires a conscious effort to do it, eventually it will lapse and be forgotten. Make a small change that becomes a habit, something that you do without thinking, and it will persist.

Celebrating Strengths shows you how to build positive habits of thought, speech and behaviour that you will keep doing and which the children will 'catch' from you, because habits are contagious.

Positive habits of thought are developed by first noticing negative thoughts, understanding why and how they occur and what the results are. The next step is to learn strategies that counter these negative thoughts. Celebrating Strengths provides games and activities that will teach both these steps and show ways of using them on a daily basis so that they become habitual.

Positive habits of speech are fostered through the emphasis on strengths and through oral story telling – the language of the strengths permeates Celebrating Strengths and is echoed in the hopeful stories being told. Soon the adults in the community will find themselves using this language without noticing they are doing it – it will have become habitual.

Positive habits of behaviour include reflection and celebration and, again, you will find practical ideas for including these vital life skills into the busy school day and helping children to do the same.

Part of the Curriculum

Celebrating Strengths uses activities, stories and celebrations that complement and support the existing curriculum – they do not require extra lessons as they meet curriculum requirements. They can be incorporated, with just a little tweaking, into what you already do, but in a way that will enhance the power, effectiveness and pleasure of your teaching and support the goals of well-being and flourishing alongside academic goals. When these approaches are embedded within your curriculum they will keep going even through staff change.

All of the activities in Celebrating Strengths meet curriculum goals – often multiple goals at the same time. For example, the activity called *Create a Story Space*, followed by *Story Telling* (explained in more detail later) can fulfil numerous objectives:

- The children are improving their listening skills – they have to listen to a story actively, especially when the story is told and there is no book to look at;
- They are using thinking skills – building the story in their heads, noticing when it is their turn to get up and help to unpack the story chest;
- They are engaged in teamwork, working in pairs or small groups, negotiating with one another, encouraging each other;
- They are making creative choices and exercising their artistic judgement as they create the story space and then select props to work with;
- They are learning about presentation skills. When they are engaged in building a Story Space each child becomes the centre of attention for a few moments, with all eyes upon them as they move and hold the stage – important skills for drama and public speaking;

- They retell a story, using traditional story language, laying the basics for better speaking and listening and for improved story writing since story telling should always precede story writing. It might be a traditional story – a literacy activity – or a story from another culture – a geography activity, or a sacred story, an RE activity.

Priming the Environment

Celebrating Strengths makes a lot of use of an under appreciated teaching aid – the physical environment. We can 'prime' our environment, fill it with positive images and positive messages, and these make a real difference to how we feel from moment to moment. The colour of our environment affects us, the sounds of the environment influence how we feel and how we work. All of these elements are used thoughtfully and deliberately within Celebrating Strengths and you will find many ideas for doing this.

Priming our environment is one example of an indirect teaching method and Celebrating Strengths works through a combination of direct and indirect teaching. The activities and assemblies provide direct teaching of strategies that improve well-being and flourishing; the environment, the stories, and the links between the festivals and the strengths provide indirect 'echoes' of those explicit messages, what I call 'sneaky teaching' – teaching without anyone realising they're being taught anything. It is very effective, especially when used in combination with direct teaching methods.

Modelling

The final teaching method used in Celebrating Strengths is modelling – in fact it underpins everything else. It is the world's most effective teaching method.

I was once asked to help someone to 'deliver' emotional literacy. How do you 'deliver' emotional literacy?? What a strange concept! Emotional literacy grows and develops through reflection and experience, through taking risks and trying new ideas, through surviving failure and moving on. It is not a lesson or a worksheet. It is a life long enterprise – I prefer the term 'emotional maturity' with its connotations of endless growth and development. My emotional maturity will, I hope, continue to grow until the day I die. We do not 'teach' emotional maturity or literacy – we live it and show it by our actions, words and responses, and encourage it daily by example and by the quality of our relationships with children and with each other.

The same is true of all the approaches and activities in Celebrating Strengths. They are not 'for children' – they are 'for people,' me and you included. They are similar to approaches used in business and in health, with the military and with managers. They have been adapted to suit children but they are based on universal principles of what helps individuals to flourish. The adults in a community will teach 'well-being' most effectively by enjoying it for themselves, they will help children to flourish by flourishing, they will encourage emotional maturity by understanding their own emotions. I use all of the tools in Celebrating Strengths in my own life, in my work and in my home and family. It is my hope that teachers will wish to do the same.

The Structure of Celebrating Strengths

Celebrating Strengths has three threads - strengths, festivals and stories, and works at three levels - that of the individual, class and whole school. You can start with any thread or any level, you can just do one thing or you can aim to do it all. To fully embed all the aspects of Celebrating Strengths will take about three years, based on the experience of the schools that have used the programme so far. Some might do it a little quicker, others take more time, but three years is broadly the right time scale to consider. Genuine change takes time.

Strengths

The underlying idea behind the emphasis on strengths is that we get more of what we focus on. Strengths are durable, fundamental qualities that describe us at our best. They are qualities like courage, kindness, persistence, curiosity and love. There is a growing awareness in business that the weakness or deficit correction model of growth is less effective than seeking to identify and build on strengths. The real potential for growth, development and success lies in your existing areas of strength. Positive psychology, a relatively new area of study that has contributed to this awareness, provides evidence for the importance of using strengths as well as cultivating positive emotion or 'happiness' and well-being. Celebrating Strengths takes these insights and applies them in schools.

I have based the strengths in Celebrating Strengths on the work of two psychologists, Chris Peterson and Martin Seligman, but have adapted their list of strengths to make it appropriate for use in schools. Teachers can test their own strengths online and observe the strengths of children. Strengths can be built and developed – they underpin good character formation. Using our strengths boosts mood and resilience, increases happiness and well-being and makes us more successful at what we do. This book gives you practical ideas for increasing your awareness and use of strengths. You get more of what you focus on, so focus on your strengths!

Celebrating Strengths links the strengths with two ancient teaching techniques, celebrating festivals and telling stories. Festivals and stories have been used to hand on values and ideas for millennia – because they work. By linking the strengths to festivals and traditional stories we ensure that these crucial ideas take deep root in the children, in us and in the school and that they outlast any changes of staff. Traditions persist and stories are memorable. Celebrating Strengths draws upon modern research into positive psychology and strengths and combines this with two ancient teaching methods, oral story telling and celebrating annual festivals.

Festivals

Celebration is a skill. In Britain, the only celebrations many people now hold are birthdays and Christmas but there is so much more in life to celebrate. You can celebrate new beginnings and endings, faith festivals or secular festivals like the first day of spring. You can celebrate who you are as a community and who we are as a world.

In past years people attended church more often and their lives were given structure and rhythm by the changing seasons of the church and the countryside. Rhythm and structure are extremely important for our mental health and we have lost much of it in modern life. The festivals in Celebrating Strengths put structure, rhythm and celebration back into the heart of school life. The festivals build happy memories, which are an important aspect of resilience, by including exciting and enjoyable whole school events as part of each one. They are also linked with certain strengths which form the focus of some of the assemblies and stories. Because of the link with festivals, all the strengths are visited each year and none are overlooked. We may enjoy using our top strengths but all the strengths are valuable and deserving of our attention. The link between the festival programme and the strengths ensures that we pay attention to each of the strengths on a regular basis.

We get more of what we focus on and all of us can grow in all of the strengths.

Stories – Strengths in Action

Stories and story telling are a very powerful teaching tool and one that is neglected in modern teacher training. I have written a whole book just on this subject alone, which you may wish to consult. The stories are one of the indirect or 'sneaky teaching' approaches in Celebrating Strengths, and are really the 'glue' that hold the festivals and the strengths together. Stories have always been integral to human celebrations, and story telling by children can be used to build literacy, speaking and listening skills, as well as providing opportunities to practice the strengths and indirect reinforcement of them.

No good story is 'about' just one thing. I dislike single subject stories – Billy Builds Self Esteem, Kitty Learns to Be Kind, that kind of thing. I don't think that is how story works. Therefore Celebrating Strengths uses traditional stories which are complex and have multiple layers of meaning. What these stories 'mean' varies from listener to listener.

The stories are not 'about' the strengths, but they do show them in action, and so I have linked stories that show certain strengths being used by particular characters to each festival. In this way the stories 'echo' the strengths that the festival is celebrating and show them in use in a fictional setting and children can notice them – or not if they wish.

Story *telling* (as opposed to reading stories aloud) enhances the power of stories enormously, and is a great tool for the personal and creative development of the teacher.

The Individual Level

At an individual level Celebrating Strengths is about each adult and each child in the community growing in awareness of their own strengths and finding new ways to use them. There are activities called Strengths Builders which, together with the stories, form part of what I call Strengths Gym. Strengths Builders are exactly what they say, activities you can use to build or exercise your strengths, like the muscle building apparatus in a gym. Some are very specific, and will just be used to build or exercise a particular strength. Others can be adapted to build or exercise most of the strengths and you can pick which strength to focus on. As you and the children learn more about the strengths you will think up new Strengths Builders and add them to your list.

The Strengths Builders are based on adult coaching tools and insights from positive psychology and executive coaching that have been adapted to work with children. You can use the 'child friendly' version or design a more adult version for yourself if you wish, though plenty of adults seem to enjoy the 'child friendly' coaching tools as much as, or sometimes more than, the 'grown up' ones! I belong to an international organisation called The Positive Workplace Alliance. When I share these activities with colleagues who are coaches, consultants, psychologists, financial advisors and CEOs, their response is always enthusiastic – and sometimes they borrow my 'child friendly' techniques for their own clients too.

Also at the individual level is the response of each person to the stories they hear and the festivals they participate in. The more you think about and tell stories, the more you use the time for reflection and celebration provided by the festivals and try out the suggestions incorporated into the assemblies, the more effective they will be.

Children can use individual Strengths Builders for themselves. You might encourage a child to use one that builds a strength you regard as valuable. They are also intended to provide additional opportunities for using top strengths because that is how you will increase enjoyment of school still further. We don't want to have to spend all our time working on things we're not good at – we all want to do more of what we really enjoy – which will be our areas of strength. If my top strength is kindness, I will positively enjoy finding new ways to use it. If my top strength is curiosity, I will thrive on extra opportunities for research. Use Strengths Builders for yourself and use them with your children.

The Class Level

Most of the Strengths Builders are designed for the whole class to do together and, again, they aim to build and exercise strengths. Some are activities that will last a full session or longer, while others take seconds. You can use them as the basis of a lesson because they meet curriculum goals, or to boost mood and prepare for a lesson. The more you incorporate them into the daily pattern of the class the more habitual they will become.

You can also, as a class, use and celebrate the festivals, work with the stories and identify the strengths in your own teaching group. You can consider the physical environment of your classroom and how it reflects each festival and the strengths you are thinking about. You can incorporate favourite stories into displays and art work. Having the strengths from the current festival on display helps draw your attention to the strengths – it 'primes the environment' and you will find yourself using the words more without thinking about it and noticing and commenting upon those strengths in the children.

You do not need to do all the Strengths Builders for each strength, nor do you need to focus on each strength for that festival (there are three strengths linked to each festival). Just pick one strength and one Strength Builder you like the look of and start with that. Follow your own enthusiasm and what you think will suit your class. Not all strengths will resonate with you and not all activities. Follow your instincts and do what you think you will all enjoy the most.

There will be stories and Strengths Builders that your class, as a whole, really respond well to. These will become part of your class *Mood Booster*, a box with suggestions for things that you all enjoy, either to improve their mood on a bad day or just to enjoy doing something you all like on a good day. Doing enjoyable activities together builds the relationships which are at the heart of Celebrating Strengths and of all good teaching. Repeat favourite stories and activities as often as you like. Children love repetition - look at how often they will watch a favourite film.

The class will also have particular strengths that you can notice and celebrate and build on. Groups have their own dynamics and their own strengths that are not quite the same as those of the individual strengths. Thinking of your class in terms of its strengths will give you a new perspective and inform your thinking and planning in a slightly different way. Getting them to decide, with you, what the class's top strengths are will also focus their attention on themselves and their peers in a new way.

There are school 'traditions' as part of each festival. You can also start 'class traditions' – things that *your* class does at the end of the week or the end of a half term. The children will enjoy these and contribute to thinking of new ones.

The Whole School Level

The whole school community consists not just of pupils and teachers of course, but includes support staff, ancillary staff, governors, parents and friends of the school. Celebrating Strengths can be enjoyed by all sections of your learning community. The more people who are involved in some way, the more effective it will be. When the whole school uses a Strengths Builder it becomes a community building activity, something that binds the community together by creating common experiences and memories, and reinforcing its shared values. The festivals incorporate these whole school Strengths Builders. Also at this level are special assemblies that celebrate and focus on the strengths of each festival and that tell stories which echo those strengths and show them in action.

The school environment can reflect the festivals, for example by associating a different colour with each one. In this way children will notice the changing seasons in the school environment. Displays can also reflect the school's emphasis on strengths. One school I work with is very skilful at weaving strengths into the captions that accompany displays. 'We used our creativity to draw these flowers', 'We made prudent choices as part of our work on Healthy Eating' and so on. If you are working on a particular strength as a school, quotes about that strength can be put up on the walls.

Story telling can be part of the life of your school, a normal way of marking occasions when you all come together and a valued part of the curriculum. The ethos of the school can be underpinned by the insights of positive psychology so that all the adults who work in the school understand the importance of focussing on strengths and of building positive emotions and a creative and positive learning environment. You can reflect together as a staff on what your strengths are as a team and on what the school's top strengths are. The children can help with this reflection and share their own insights, too.

Getting Started

There are practical activities at the end of each chapter for you to try for yourself, first, and then to use at a staff meeting to introduce other staff to the concepts within the book. An important principle is that the activities, all of them Strengths Builders, are meant to be enjoyable because enjoyment matters. But that does not mean they are easy! You will need to use your strengths of persistence and courage as well as considerable creativity and the more you use them the stronger they grow.

Another important principle of Celebrating Strengths is that we practice what we preach. We don't 'deliver' emotional literacy, we live it. We don't just tell the children they have strengths, we are aware of strengths in ourselves and in everyone we meet. The Strengths Builders at the end of each chapter are for you to try out and see if they work. Change them by all means because they need to suit you and your way of working but try them out for yourself and see. Then, if you want to become a Strengths Champion in your school there are training ideas to use with colleagues at staff meetings or training days. You can introduce colleagues to Strengths Builders and introduce the children to them too.

Start small and make a single change, tell a single story, use a single Strengths Builder and remember that small changes add up and that teachers change the world.

Strengths Builder: WWW
(Use to build hope, persistence, gratitude, modesty)

WWW stands for What Went Well? Start using it yourself at the end of a day and at the end of a week as a professional development tool. Draw WWW in the middle of a page and begin to doodle all the positives you can think of – the more you do this the easier it becomes. Even bad days have some good things in them. Reflecting on what has gone well allows you to build on successes and develop them.

Training Idea: WWW

Explain to colleagues that WWW is used to counter what psychologists call negative bias – our tendency to spot easily the things that go wrong. This was an evolutionary advantage during human development – those who spotted and remembered dangers and potential hazards survived. Now, however, it has less advantage and can lead to depression.

Teaching our brain to counter its natural negative bias can make us more optimistic, more successful and healthier.

As an exercise, take the previous week or half term and notice what has gone well. This starts off being quite difficult – remember, this is normal. Once you make a start, however, it gets gradually easier and easier and soon you will have collected a host of positive memories.

Exercises like WWW build on what has been called the 'neuroplasticity' of the brain i.e. its ability to grow and change into old age. Every positive thought creates a channel in the brain. Lots of positive thoughts create deeper, stronger channels that consequently make positive thought easier. The same is true, of course, of negative thought. The aim of WWW is to build positive pathways in the brain.

TWO

Positive Psychology in Education

AN OLD AND WISE FRIEND, Tony Datkiewicz, said to me on my wedding day, 'Store up the happy memories, Jenny, against the bad times.' He knew it to be true from experience and I have found it to be so, too. There is now research to show that Tony was right. My grandmother, and yours too, I'm sure, told us to count our blessings. Studies now show that doing exactly that can have a significant effect on reducing depression and increasing happiness.

This research is coming from a field called positive psychology, a relatively recent development in the field of mental health. It has been championed in particular by the American psychologist Martin Seligman. He argued that alongside the essential work of treating and studying mental illness, psychology should also study human well-being, strengths and potential, and look at talented and flourishing individuals as well as those who are struggling.

Positive psychology studies areas like contentment, hope, optimism, pleasure and engagement. It focuses on positive traits such as love, courage and creativity, and virtues like citizenship, tolerance and responsibility. It looks at 'outstanding' individuals and asks how is it that they function so well? It also looks at 'average' people and asks what is right, what is working well and what is getting better?

Positive psychology brings scientific rigour and experiment to the field of human flourishing and a framework that draws together previously unconnected ideas and intuitions. Good teachers have always known that a cheerful class is easier to teach – now there are scientific studies that show that this is true *and* that cheerful children learn more effectively. So you can now legitimately spend the first five minutes of a lesson playing a game to put the children in a good mood and then inform anyone who queries this that what you are doing is in accord with Fredrickson's 'broaden-and-build' theory of positive emotions and is as educationally sound as it gets! Positive psychology brings scientific tools to the study of what makes people flourish and the important effects of positive emotion. It provides insights and ideas that are of use, not just to teachers, but to anyone who works with people.

Building Positive Habits

Positive psychology can help us, as individuals and as a community, to build positive habits of thought, speech and behaviour. Firstly in ourselves, and then in the children we work with.

We get more of what we focus on. If we habitually focus on weakness and remedying weaknesses then we will struggle to help children to flourish. Conversely, if we focus on strengths we will find and help them to develop even further. If I had to spend all day and everyday trying to programme computers I would be miserable – I get cross enough trying to work out how my new email system functions! It is just *not* what I am good at or enjoy doing. I have to learn how to do it, but the last thing I want to do is spend *most* of my time and energy on computers and their systems – I would not be successful, I would not be happy, I would not flourish. No matter how long I spend at computing, it will never become a strength, never be an area I truly excel in. The most I can aim for is coping, or competence, at being 'all right' at it.

Positive psychology makes the basic point that removing weakness is not the same as building strengths and helping people to flourish and to excel. If you draw a line from -5 to +5 then conventional psychology (and possibly much of education) aims to fix weakness, to move us from -5 to 0, where 0 represents OK or 'alright' or 'coping'. What they do not do is help us reach +5, the realm of flourishing.

-5	0	+5
Weakness	neutral	flourishing

As a teacher (and as a parent) I am not interested in whether children are 'alright' or whether they 'are coping'. I am not primarily interested, even, in fixing their weaknesses though some of the time I do need to do this. What I really want to know is, are they flourishing, are they reaching their potential, are they using their strengths and building on them, can they identify and follow their passions and learn how to make a difference to the world? Remedying weakness is *not the same* as helping children to excel, to flourish, to achieve their potential. Remedying weakness gets children to OK. It is important but not enough. It is finding children's strengths and then, crucially, giving them ample opportunities to use those strengths that will help them to flourish, and flourishing is at the core of what education is about.

We get more of what we focus on - which means, also, that the very questions we raise, the very issues we look at create and affect our reality. If we focus on poor behaviour we will find poor behaviour; if we put our time and energy into poor results our horizons will be bounded by poor results. A study into the low achievement of children in inner cities in America found that this was caused by family breakdown, poverty, poor education, drug abuse – nothing surprising there. A rather different study asked not, why do so many children in inner cities fail, but why do some children from inner cities succeed? It looked at the key concept of resilience and found that features such as social support, optimism, a sense of meaning, a focus on strengths and goal setting helped children from difficult backgrounds to excel.

Positive psychology helps us form the habit of asking different questions, not how do I fix this problem, but how do I achieve more flourishing and excellence? How do I get more of that excellent lesson, that brilliant behaviour? What do I enjoy in my teaching and how do I get more of it?

Is Happiness Important?

Aristotle is quoted a great deal by positive psychologists. He said that happiness was the highest good, the only thing we pursue for its own end. We seek everything else – love, friendship, money, power, in order, he said, to be happy. Happiness is clearly an important subject but is it an appropriate concern for teachers?

Psychologists are beginning to be able to measure the effects of happiness, sometimes called, more scientifically, well-being or even 'subjective well-being'. These effects include longer life, happy marriages, better physical health and protection from negative life events. Being happy much of the time does not stop bad things happening to us but it does mean we tend to bounce back quicker from the difficulties that we encounter.

In the classroom, too, happiness has some very specific and important effects. Fashions change within education. In centuries past it was thought that fear was a good motivator for learning. Thankfully that idea lost favour but it has been replaced by a rather neutral approach – learning may be boring but it is good for you so you have to do it. Now psychologists recognise that effective learning is linked to happiness and enjoyment and that the happiest and most optimistic among us are also those who learn most efficiently and who go furthest both academically and in other areas of life.

Positive emotions produce cognitive changes. Studies show that feeling happy results in a rise in our ability to pay attention and to notice what is happening around us. It gives us a better working memory, more verbal fluency and an increased openness to information. In the classroom, while I strongly resist the idea that children need constant entertaining or 'fun' in a shallow sense, I am forced by the evidence to accept that humour, zest, enjoyment and what we might term 'buzz' facilitates learning. Happy children are the children who are most open and able to learn.

There are three areas that Seligman highlights as being essential to happiness and well-being. They have to do with our feelings about the past, the present and the future. These are happy memories, flow, and hope or optimism. They are all highly relevant to education. We can use all three to improve learning in the classroom and our own enjoyment of teaching.

Happy Memories

Our feelings about the past can dramatically affect how we feel and function in the present. Ruminating on past wrongs, noticing only what we lack or have lacked, resentment or sadness about missed opportunities, despair about past failures - all have very real effects in the here and now. On a day to day level in the classroom, the child who remembers only what they got wrong yesterday and who fails to pay equal or greater attention to what they got right will be less resilient and less persistent when struggling with the challenges of today. Helping children to notice the positive aspects in each day and reframing 'failure' as a necessary and positive part of learning is essential if they are to flourish and reach their potential.

Fostering happy memories is a skill – a positive habit - and it is one we can build and use in the classroom. One of the reasons I have worked to help schools create enjoyable festivals is the fact that happy memories are part of what makes us resilient – they are like a store-house of hope that can take us through the bad times, as my friend Tony said. Encouraging children to stop and notice enjoyable experiences and focus on them so that they can recall them in detail provides them with a rich inner resource to take into later life. Celebrating Strengths sets out quite deliberately to build happy memories in children to improve their resilience and enjoyment of life.

Memory is a powerful tool. Recalling a happy event, perhaps a time we laughed and laughed, suggests to our mind and body that we feel that happy *now* and this produces chemical changes, a release of endorphins, in the present. Knowing that this is the case and practising recall of happy memories, as in the Strengths Builder *Pearls*, teaches children that they are not helpless victims of their emotions, but that there are things they can do to improve their mood.

This is also of relevance for purely academic reasons. Seligman quotes an experiment in which children were given a maths test. They were divided into three groups and one group took the test at once. Another group were given an unexpected piece of chocolate and then took the maths test. A third group were asked to think of a time they were so happy they jumped up and down with joy and then they took the maths test. The second and third groups did better on the test. The pleasure that comes from remembering a happy time is a powerful classroom tool.

How do we look back on failures and bad events? Setbacks in life are inevitable and they are uncomfortable. What matters to our long term success is what we do with those setbacks. Do we learn from them, pick ourselves up and carry on or do we give up? Which path we choose is greatly influenced by how we explain those setbacks to ourselves and whether these explanations are predominantly pessimistic or optimistic. What are the stories we tell ourselves when things go wrong? Psychologists call this kind of story telling 'explanatory style'.

Imagine I am running late for work because my car failed to start. My pessimistic thoughts start working overtime. 'I'm going to be late. This always happens. Now the client will think I'm unreliable and cancel the training day. Word will get round, I may never work again, the children will starve, the house will fall down, we'll catch pneumonia and DIE!!' You recognise the pattern because we all do it – I do it particularly well! What matters is whether we *mostly* do this or whether our thinking runs more along the following, more realistic lines: 'I'm going to be late – that's not good. But I can ring ahead and warn them. I am usually very reliable. I have never been late before. This once I'll just have to apologise, we all have bad days, I'm human!' The two stories leave us feeling very different – the same event, but explained to ourselves in a different light and with very different emotional outcomes.

If we mostly tell ourselves negative stories and use more pessimistic explanations it will undermine our ability to keep going in the face of setback, to look forward optimistically. Left unchecked this can even lead to depression and much unhappiness. What is really important about this for teachers is that children mirror the explanatory style of the adults around them. If children hear adults saying, 'typical, this always happens to me, nothing ever works round here, nobody cares etc' then they will start to use these kind of 'stories' for themselves. Such stories, very simply, undermine their ability to learn and to achieve their academic potential.

It is really important that we practice telling ourselves positive stories and building positive habits of thought for ourselves – because positive habits are contagious and these are what we want to pass on to the children we work with. I will introduce you in Chapter 6 to *Eeyore Thoughts*, a Strengths Builder that helps you and the children to build positive habits of thought.

Prepare and Repair

We have already seen how feeling cheerful affects learning. This means that unhappy children will not learn as effectively. It is therefore important then that we think of ways to help children to prepare for learning. We prepare the room, we prepare our teaching materials but if they (or we!) are cross or tired or hot and bothered, our teaching and their learning will be less effective. Happy memories, a short Strengths Builder like *Pearls* can be used to prepare for learning. You might tell a joke or show a brief funny video clip. Laughter really improves mood.

Quieter souls among us need to work out how to boost mood at the start of lessons if we are really not capable of – or temperamentally suited to - the song and dance routine. I do use jokes but I have other, quieter methods of raising enjoyment levels and for calming children if they seem over stimulated. Story telling is one of them – I have yet to meet a child or adult who did not love listening to a story. I also use stillness and silence to create wonder and pleasure and relaxation –

light a candle, darken the room. Occasional and unexpected pieces of chocolate (I happen to think that occasional chocolate IS part of a healthy diet!) also work wonders – give them out before a test. Remember, the results showed that students who received an unexpected piece of chocolate before a maths test out performed those who did not.

All of the Strengths Builders in Celebrating Strengths are meant to be enjoyed. Introducing activities that children enjoy into the classroom to **prepare** for learning is as essential a part of teaching as providing them with pencils and paper and teaching them the alphabet.

Such activities can also used to **repair** when things go wrong, when we loose our cool, blow our top or when it has been a bad tempered grumpy day all round. That is human and natural – but it doesn't help us to teach well, or the children to learn well. So, *Pearls* and other Strengths Builders will help you to **prepare and repair**.

Flow

Preparing for learning in this way encourages what psychologists call optimal functioning or 'flow'. 'Flow' has been written about a great deal by the wonderfully named psychologist Mihaly Csikszentmihalyi, (pronounced Cheeks Sent Me High). It is an important concept for teachers to understand and use. Csikszentmihalyi studied artists working at full capacity and noticed how oblivious they were to hunger or fatigue and how strongly self motivated they were – working not for money or recognition but because they had a deep inner need and desire to do what they were doing. Flow is defined as a sense of deep engagement during which time passes quickly and the person is working at full capacity – nothing distracts us and we learn, grow and make progress towards our goal. During flow there is no great sense of self – it is emotionally a rather neutral state because the focus is so completely on the task at hand. However the aftermath of flow is invigorating – afterwards the person feels happy and relaxed with a sense of achievement. I know when I'm in flow, often when writing, because my tea goes cold and I am late to pick my son up from school!

Flow is what happens when we work at full capacity, either at play or at work but usually at something we have chosen to do. The psychologist Chris Peterson argues that flow is rarely experienced by pupils during any school activity, perhaps because most of their tasks lack that crucial aspect of choice. I happen to think he is overly pessimistic but it is a challenge for all teachers to consider.

In my experience children, especially younger children, do achieve flow in school but perhaps not as often as we might wish. Young children enter flow very naturally during play and will play for hours, learning and growing, oblivious to what is happening around them. Translating that absorption into a more formal learning setting is a challenge but how wonderful it would be if we could create classrooms in which there were ever more frequent opportunities for flow, for full functioning, to occur. What would a 'flow friendly' classroom look like?

Flow occurs not when we are masters of a subject but when there is a good balance between skill and challenge – too little challenge and we are bored, too much and we feel anxious or frustrated. Teachers who are skilled at judging that level for each child and who can encourage them to follow their own interests in their work will be those most able to help children to achieve flow, to function to their full capacity. We need to challenge them – hard work is challenging and you don't achieve flow if you are bored – but we also need to make sure they are comfortable with making mistakes and not anxious about failure. We need to push them out of their comfort zones and into their stretch zone because that is where flow and optimal functioning and most learning happens. Of course they can't stay in their stretch zones all day and every day and neither can we but the more they do achieve flow the happier and more successful they will feel!

There are, as yet, no tools for measuring flow in the classroom – it would be an excellent project to develop a way of assessing just how much engagement is happening during a lesson because it is when children are engaged, when they are in flow, that they are learning and it is when teachers are in flow that they are teaching at their optimum.

I am interested in the links between meditation and flow. Meditation is a highly focussed kind of attention. I have developed what I would broadly call 'meditative activities' as a way of starting lessons which may encourage subsequent flow. These are calming, focussing exercises that can last as little as 30 seconds but which allow children to gather themselves before the task at hand. Athletes accept and work on the importance of mental preparation before they compete so that they enter the 'zone' when they need to. Teachers and pupils will also benefit from mental preparation for the task of learning. Some of the Strengths Builders, like *Rain Stick Listening*, are explicitly designed as simple meditative preparations for work. Others, like *Create a Story Space*, incorporate an element of focussing and calming within them.

Stretch Zones, Failure and Self Esteem

We learn when we are outside our comfort zones. That is where we experience flow, but also fear. I am indebted to the psychologist Tal Ben-Shahar for the concept of 'stretch zones'. It is when we move out of our comfort zone into our stretch zones that we learn and grow and develop. But that involves tolerating a certain amount of fear and consequently the exercise of courage. We learn when we are challenged, not when we are totally comfortable, we develop when we master these challenges, not when we avoid them. Outside our stretch zone there is a panic zone and we don't really learn there either – we might, with a lot of courage, survive there for a little while, but not for long. I tell children that if they find themselves in their panic zone it is vital that they ask for help, and it is the job of the adults around them to help them back into their stretch zones.

Comfort zone   **Stretch** zone (learning/self esteem/courage)   **Panic** zone (ask for help/courage)

It is the exercise of courage that is at the core of building self esteem. Failing should not damage self esteem, failing is essential if we are to learn and grow. I would not, as some educationalists have suggested, eliminate the word failure from the dictionary and replace it with 'deferred success'. I prefer to redefine 'failure' as an important and essential part of learning and an indicator that we are working in our stretch zones, as we should be. Failing is not the problem. It is the habit of giving up and retreating to our comfort zones that can damage self esteem.

As Tal Ben-Shahar says frequently, 'learn to fail or fail to learn'. For children, it is essential that we send the message that any failure on their part is normal, expected, and even welcome because it means that they are extending themselves. It is also crucial that they feel their failure is shared with us. If they fail, it is *our* problem, not their problem, and one we can solve together – children should not feel left alone with failure.

It is also important to consider what we mean by 'success.' If, by success, we mean straight A*s and a place at Cambridge, relatively few will succeed. Success should mean doing our best and using our strengths to make the world a better place. A school caretaker who loves their work and their community is making the world a better place. I know several superb caretakers who make an incredibly important contribution to the children's learning and happiness and to the community to which they belong. Academic prowess is not the only thing we should value even in schools.

It is crucial to praise effort and perseverance and courage as much as, if not more than we praise actual results. Today I may get A's but tomorrow, with the same effort, on a harder paper, I may get only B's. If I think I have to get A's to earn your good opinion, I may feel anxious and even give up. If I know I earn that good opinion by showing effort and courage, then I feel secure that I can do that just as well tomorrow.

We build self esteem when we exercise courage, when we push ourselves outside our comfort zones and keep going until we do succeed. That requires effort and courage and persistence – our role as teachers is to provide encouragement and recognition of those qualities when we see them. That recognition is actually much more valuable to pupils than stickers or rewards – they want our praise, our good opinion, a smile to let them know we care about them. Encouragement, which is closely linked to courage and has the same root word, 'cor' or heart, is key to the teaching role – acknowledging them, helping them to reflect on their own work and abilities, and recognising the effort they make, being appreciative of co-operative, helpful actions.

Hope and Optimism

Education is, or should be, all about hope, as well as courage. It is preparation for the future, time spent learning now in the belief that what is learnt will help pupils to grow and flourish in later life. Teachers need to be hopeful people because if we have no hope for our pupils they will certainly have no hope for themselves. Optimistic children show more persistence in tasks and achieve more academic success than children lacking in optimism. Building optimism is therefore a key aspect of education. Seligman argues that optimistic thinking is a skill that can be learned and I have incorporated his insights into some of the Strengths Builders.

Optimism is part of what makes children and adults resilient. Resilient people bounce back from the setbacks of life. Resilient children experience deprivation or trauma in childhood but go on to be happy and successful adults. Other features of resilient people are the ability to notice and control their own emotions, a good sense of self esteem and a belief in their ability to make a difference to their lives and to achieve what they set out to achieve. Resilient people can think clearly about their strengths and weaknesses, their successes and setbacks and they both feel a need for and are able to build good relationships with others. These are all skills that can be taught and improved.

Another feature of resilient people, as has already been mentioned, is their ability to store happy memories against the hard times. Here is a way of beginning such a 'store'. It can be developed into a Strengths Builder called *Treasure Chest*. A Treasure Chest is a box or an album of happy memories. Each person can have an individual Treasure Chest, or there can be one for the whole class. When you have a really good experience, you write about it, draw it, take a photo to remind you of it, or just imprint the memory into a Pearl as explained below. You put the notes, or drawings, or photos into your Treasure Chest and, when you are low or wish to be inspired, you open it up and savour the good experiences all over again.

Strengths Builder: Pearls
(Use to build gratitude, hope and self control)

Put some quiet, soothing music on and find yourself some pastels and a sheet of paper. Close your eyes and start to recall a happy memory, a 'pearl', perhaps from a recent holiday or further back if you wish. Create the memory as clearly as you can in your mind, making it detailed and colourful. It is as if you are making a film of the event in your mind. Then you step right inside it and re-experience the film, the happy memory from the inside. Notice your surroundings, the weather, your feelings; smile to yourself as this increases your positive feelings even more.

Opening your eyes, start to play with the pastels, reproducing the colours of your memory film, the shapes, not worrying about accurate drawing but doodling in colour as you continue to dwell on the memory.

As you complete this event, after five or ten minutes, notice any changes in your energy and mood levels.
You can keep your art work as a record of your happy memory – you might call it a pearl picture. Put it on your desk while teaching. Glancing at it will bring back some of those positive feelings.

Training Idea: Pearls

Pearls is a good opening activity for any staff meeting. You can use it demonstrate to colleagues the powerful effect in the present of happy memories. You can also do it at the start of the year to ensure that everyone has a *pearl picture* to keep on their desk.

THREE

Strengths and Strengths Gym

What are Strengths?

STRENGTHS ARE CAPACITIES to think, feel and behave in certain ways. They represent what is best about us and when we use our strengths we are energised, we sparkle and soar, we achieve the highest goals we are capable of achieving. All cultures and faiths recognise certain human strengths and there is nearly universal agreement about what the core strengths and virtues are, about what it is that makes a good person, a good citizen. Of course there are important differences between cultures and faiths but our common ground, what we agree on is the importance of strengths such as kindness, hope, courage and creativity. The strengths have also been called 'values' because they are things that are good, that represent the best in human beings. Here is the list of strengths that we use in Celebrating Strengths. This list has been developed and adapted from the VIA Classification of Strengths that was put together by Christopher Peterson and Martin Seligman.

- creativity
- love of learning
- openness
- wisdom
- enthusiasm
- persistence
- courage
- honesty
- fairness
- teamwork
- leadership
- love
- kindness
- friendship
- generosity
- gratitude
- spirituality
- humour
- hope
- love of beauty
- forgiveness
- prudence
- self control
- modesty
- patience.

We all have all of these qualities to some degree but we will possess some more than others. Those we have most of can be called our 'top strengths'. It is when adults use these top strengths that they experience the greatest sense of personal fulfilment, enjoy the greatest success and feel happiest. It is also in the area of our top strengths that we have the greatest capacity to grow and develop – in other words, to flourish. A day spent using our top strengths is a happy, energising and fulfilling day. A day when we have not been able to use any of our top strengths will be experienced as dull, frustrating and draining.

The same is true of children, which is why Celebrating Strengths encourages both adults and children to become increasingly aware of their top strengths and to use them as much as they can. The strengths are looked at in much more detail in Part Three on the festivals.

What about Weaknesses?

A great deal of education (and business too) is based on what is called a 'deficit model', finding out what is wrong and fixing it. Positive psychology calls for a shift in the balance, a move away from focussing on what is wrong with us, to focussing much more on what is right with us and doing more of it. When children are working on what they are weakest at they will become tired more easily, more easily frustrated and they may experience a lack of confidence. When they are using their top strengths in some capacity they will build their confidence and self esteem, achieve the best that they can achieve and enjoy life and school and learning.

Clearly we cannot just engage with activities that employ our top strengths all the time – I may be dyslexic but I still need to learn to spell at a basic level. However, a life spent concentrating on spelling will undermine and frustrate me – using my strengths as much as I can will give me the energy and confidence to tackle what I'm not so good at.

All the strengths are important. We benefit from using our top strengths as much as possible but we do also benefit from developing the other strengths because they are all important aspects of being human. Forgiveness, for example, may not be high on my personal list of strengths but it is a very important aspect of life. A lack of forgiveness can lead to years of bitterness and unhappiness. I may never become a paragon of forgiveness, it will not soar into my top five strengths, but I will still benefit from spending time reflecting on it, thinking about people who have used it in exemplary ways, cultivating it in my own life. I can build this strength so that even though it may never become a top strength, I can still have more of it.

Because all of the strengths are important, the strengths are linked to regular annual festivals within Celebrating Strengths. Because we celebrate the festivals each year, we will spend time thinking about all the strengths each year. I will probably enjoy most the festival that has most of my top strengths attached to it – I will find in it plenty of opportunities to use my top strengths and to sparkle. But I will also grow and develop through the other festivals as they focus on other important strengths. I may surprise myself by finding an unexpected affinity for strengths I didn't really consider to be 'me' at all. I may relish the challenge of using a strength I know I don't really have much of at all!

Changing our Perceptions

In life, and in education, we get more of what we focus on. Notice children's weaknesses and you will see them all around you. Focus on the children's strengths and you will find more and more evidence of them. This can be really helpful with challenging children. We have all worked with children who, troubled themselves, seek to trouble us and pass on their unhappiness. We may struggle to find anything positive to say about such children at the end of a difficult day. The concept and language of strengths can help enormously here. One very good teacher was struggling with a boy who constantly challenged her, argued with her and his peers and generally told everyone what to do and how to do it. Having been working with the strengths for some time she turned to me and said, 'What can you do? He's a born leader! We need leaders.' The language of the strengths can be really helpful in allowing us to positively reframe how we see more challenging pupils. Are they disruptive or is vitality and enthusiasm so much their top strength they struggle to contain them?

I worked with a boy, very disruptive for his teacher, whose love for his parents was at the heart of his difficulties at school. He wanted to fix life for them and could not. It was his top strength – caring and loving – that was leading him to feel so angry and then to behave in a way that disrupted lessons. Seeing that strength does not change his behaviour, nor does it make it acceptable, but it may subtly change how we feel about and subsequently relate to such a child. Saying, 'You clearly love your family very much, you show so much care for them' may in fact alter a child's self perception enough to lead to change.

Sharing with parents our insights and thoughts about their children's strengths can give parents additional tools for building self esteem in their children – a new and very positive language for speaking with them. It may also alter how they see their children. 'Your child cannot sit still' sends one message. 'Your child has so much enthusiasm and energy' sends a rather different one.

Strengths in Education

Some adults find it hard to identify and talk about their strengths. It seems boastful. It is not really boastful, however, but grateful, to look at ourselves and to see and wonder at what our ancestors, our parents, our experiences, our beliefs and cultural heritage, and our hard work have made us. True humility knows what it's good at. Paradoxically perhaps, the more aware I am of my strengths, and the more I use them, the more comfortable I become with admitting to myself and others, those areas I am less good at.

Sharing with parents the strengths we see and value in their child may make them more open and able to hear about the areas that the child is not so good at without the attendant anxiety that such news often brings.

There are insights from strengths research that are important for education. A recent study of US newly qualified teachers showed that teachers high in the strengths of enthusiasm and humour had classes that out performed those of teachers without those particular strengths. Laughter, fun, zest – all of these things don't just add to our enjoyment of the classroom, they add to the effectiveness with which our children learn, too. When teachers are using their own top strengths they will enjoy their teaching more, feel more fulfilled and engaged by what they do and transmit that enthusiasm to their pupils. Awareness of our strengths, and using them more, makes sense for both children and adults alike.

Love of learning is, of course, one of the most vital strengths for teachers to possess and to transmit and encourage in their pupils. Schools where learning is seen as an exciting Adventure – and a pleasure - by most of the adults present will naturally foster a life long love of learning in their pupils. Schools where teachers are, themselves, still learning either professionally or personally are going to be excellent schools. It doesn't really matter if you are learning more about your favourite subject, about new teaching techniques or line dancing – as long as you are learning something and the children know it. Studying just to pass exams – focussing too much on grades and achievement, rather than encouraging a love of learning for its own sake, will inevitably undermine the development of this vital strength. Letting teachers and pupils follow their interests and enthusiasms – to learn just for the pleasure of learning, to master skills for the thrill of mastery and not for an A* grade, will foster life long enthusiasm for learning.

It is not only individuals who have top strengths – groups have them too. It can be immensely affirming for staff teams to consider what top strengths they possess as a group. Are there omissions they could fill? Where do they excel? What about the school as a whole? What are the top strengths of your particular learning community? It can subtly change our perception of ourselves to realise and affirm that, 'This school's top strengths are love, kindness and a love of learning' or 'We have the top strengths of open mindedness, creativity and love of learning'. Displayed in an entrance hall these would make excellent mission statements for any school. Letting children consider and give their opinions about the school's strengths would be an invaluable part of the process of drawing up such a mission statement.

Strengths Gym

Strengths Gym is an important part of Celebrating Strengths. It consists of two elements, one direct, another indirect, a 'sneaky teaching' method. The direct elements of Strengths Gym are the Strengths Builders. In a gym you have machines for toning and for building muscle. Strengths Builders are the 'machines' of Strengths Gym, games, activities and suggestions for using each of the strengths. If, for example at the festival of performing arts, we are focussing on courage and this is one of your top strengths, then a Strengths Builder for courage, like the *Courage Meditation* will give you ideas for using and thinking about courage even more, for exercising that 'muscle' and keeping it honed, as though in a gym. If courage is not a top strength you can use the Strengths Builders to build that particular muscle and make it bigger.

Teachers can use Strengths Builders for themselves, can encourage children to use them individually and can use them as a class activity for everyone to join in.

The indirect elements of Strengths Gym are the traditional stories that echo the strengths of the festival. They are not, as I have said elsewhere, 'about' a particular strength but they contain characters who show examples of the strengths in action. By doing so, they affirm, indirectly, the children's own strengths and the strengths of the festival.

All of the Strengths Builders and the stories are helping to build positive habits of thought, speech and behaviour.

Some strengths are more associated with life satisfaction than others so it makes sense to place particular emphasis on Strengths Builders that allow children to practice and build those strengths – gratitude, love, vitality, curiosity and hope are all strengths that tend to make us happier. Encouraging the development of these strengths, together with identifying the other strengths that children possess, will be key factors in a rounded education.

The Strengths Builders are taken from positive psychology and the field of coaching. Some of them are adaptations of the kind of activities that coaches suggest to their clients, whether those clients are leaders of business and industry or individuals who want to flourish and lead more successful lives. If leaders in industry find coaching exercises helpful and relevant – and increasingly they do – then children have a right to share in the insights of this emerging field. Celebrating Strengths is a strengths-based coaching tool for schools.

Strengths Builders can be used by individuals and by the whole class and some will adapt for use in assemblies too. Assemblies are a time to focus on the particular strengths of *this* festival, for thinking together as a school about the strengths and what they look like in practice. It is also a good time for inviting children for whom that is a top strength to act as leaders, during this festival, helping the rest of us by giving us ideas for using the strengths and setting an example. It is important that children for whom these are top strengths are encouraged to take the lead in this way.

Strengths and Resilience

There is a large overlap between strengths and resilience. The elements of resilience, optimism, emotional literacy, self control and self efficacy, fit well with particular strengths. Knowing how to control and manage one's own emotions, for example, is an important part of the strength of friendship – it is what makes us a good friend to others and to ourselves and it is a part of self control, too. Self efficacy, believing in our ability to achieve things and make changes, is an aspect of hope or optimism. Self control is a separate strength in its own right.

Since these skills can be taught and contribute immensely to life success, they are part of education in its broadest sense. A resilient child will persist in the face of setbacks, will form good relationships with peers and adults and will probably flourish in educational and other settings. Such skills are as much a part of learning and preparing for life as the skills of reading and writing and therefore as much part of a teacher's concern. Indeed, just as 'soft' skills often make the difference in the work place between success and failure, so too they are a vital part of education at all levels. These skills are incorporated into the Strengths Builders and all of them, besides building resilience, meet curriculum goals at the same time.

The festivals also reinforce the skills of resilience. For example, the ability to relax is an important element of controlling our emotions –

being able to recognise how we are feeling and knowing what to do to improve our mood if it is low, or calm ourselves down if we are angry or over wrought. All of the festivals include Strengths Builders that are actually meditations or opportunities for quiet and reflection – it is in quietness that we can begin to notice ourselves and our emotions, while meditation has been shown to improve mood as well as the ability to relax and control ourselves.

There are numerous Strengths Builders for each strength and concept because I want teachers to follow their own strengths and enthusiasms in implementing them. Do not try to do everything, do not do an activity that makes you yawn just reading it. Choose one that sparks your interest or which suggests an adaptation immediately to your mind. Follow your enthusiasm because it is by your enthusiasm that you will teach most effectively. The Strengths Builders need to suit *you*, first, and then your class for them to be effective. If you enjoy an activity you will persist with it until it becomes a natural part of your repertoire, something you 'always' do. It will have become a positive habit, of thought, or speech or behaviour.

Practice What We Preach

Celebrating Strengths is a coaching tool for the whole community, **not** something we 'deliver' to the children. The principles behind it are ones that we work on in our own lives. It is not something we 'deliver' or really teach, come to that via a lesson plan and target objectives. The Strengths Builders may be 'child friendly' – they are designed to be accessible at many levels – but they are certainly not meant just for children but for everyone.

I use these tools in my daily life all the time. I use them with adult coaching clients and with groups of professionals with whom I work.

Teachers need to try out the tools and use them for themselves before they begin to introduce them to children. If you find you often explain setbacks in a pessimistic manner, for example, trying to encourage children to have a more optimistic outlook by using a Strengths Builder like *Eeyore Thoughts* will simply not work. You will be saying one thing but doing another. Try out *Eeyore Thoughts* for yourself first, notice how you explain bad events to yourself, practice being more realistic in your own thinking. Having done this, you will then be better able to model optimistic thinking for the children and it will become a natural part of your classroom and their emotional environment. When a more Tigger like thinking style has become habitual for you, it will become habitual for the children you work with.

Strengths Builder: My top strengths
(Use to build modesty, gratitude and enthusiasm, friendship, spirituality and self control)

Sit down with the list of strengths and decide, for yourself, which five you think you use the most.

Then set aside 40 minutes to do the online VIA strengths assessment. (**www.authentichappiness.org**)

Compare the two lists. Which do you think is the most authentic YOU?

Training Idea: Whose strengths are these?

This is a great team building exercise. Ask colleagues to either self select their top five strengths or to do the VIA strengths test – but not to share the results with anybody. Then everyone types their five top strengths onto a sheet of paper, without their name on it and puts it in a box.

The box is unpacked onto a table, and staff have to try to match the lists of top five strengths with their colleagues.

The discussions that ensue can be powerfully supportive and give an opportunity for us to voice positive thoughts about one another that we are usually too reticent to share.

Finally, each person claims their own sheet and colleagues can comment on which other key strengths they observe in addition to that person's top five strengths.

FOUR

Stories and Story Telling

STORIES AND STORY TELLING are an essential part of Celebrating Strengths. They are the golden thread that weaves its way through all the festivals. They bind the strengths to the celebrations and provide space for the strengths to breathe life into the curriculum. They show the strengths in action. Stories provide magic and metaphor, space for the children to reflect on their own strengths in the light of ancient tales, space to find their own strengths affirmed and re affirmed. They become old, enduring, and memorable friends.

Story telling is one of two ancient teaching techniques used in Celebrating Strengths to ensure that the concepts of the strengths and other positive ideas take deep and lasting root within individuals, classrooms and schools. Long after the content of any lesson on PSHE has been forgotten, children will remember 'Werberga was a saint, everybody said so, and they told stories about her kindness,' or 'Caedmon took a deep breath, summoned all his courage and sang' or 'Sita kept her promises, so can we.' This is because stories are memorable and stories last - for hundreds of years! Linking stories to the strengths, indirectly, means the children's awareness of the strengths, their strengths, will last too. Stories are a crucial part of Celebrating Strengths – they are the indirect reinforcement that balances the direct work of the Strengths Builders and they show the strengths in action. They, too, are building positive habits of thought, speech and behaviour.

Stories – An Indirect and Respectful Teaching Tool

Stories work indirectly, or at least they should. Stories are the ultimate 'sneaky teaching' tool. Stories, good stories, are complex, multi-layered tales. I use a lot of traditional tales, ancient stories hundreds of years old. They have lasted hundreds of years because they are good stories, because they speak to many people on many different levels. They are not 'about' any one thing but it is possible to find meaning within them, and often many meanings.

A story does not say 'do this, do that, be this, be that'. It is far more subtle than that. It paints a world and invites you to enter it, to identify first with this character, then with that character, to wonder what will happen, to *care* what will happen and finally to decide for yourself what it means, what it says to you. Stories clearly teach as well. All the great religious leaders used stories to teach. However, they are not didactic, they do not preach. Rather, they offer an idea and the listener can take it, or leave it, or interpret it another way. They do not say, 'be kind,' they say, 'here is a tale about a boy who showed kindness to a lion and this is what happened to him.........What do YOU think?' Stories are a profoundly respectful teaching technique because they allow us to say no to what is being taught.

Like all people, listeners are actually more likely to take on board a meaning or message if they are given the option *not* to accept it. If the listener then chooses to identify with a meaning or message they can see in the story, that meaning or message will take root much more deeply because the listener has chosen to accept it – it has not been forced upon them.

It is for this reason that I am not, it has to be said, a great fan of stories written to illustrate a single point or theme, such as the 'Johnny has to go to the doctor,' or 'Anne's parents divorce,' or even, 'Jack builds self esteem' school of storytelling. The object is laudable but unless they are first and foremost good stories children will not enjoy them. My objection is partly, that this genre contains stories of a very mixed standard and children should be offered only the very best art and literature. The world abounds in rich, ancient, complex tales and we honestly don't need to write 'Jack builds self esteem' when we have a wonderful story about Jack chopping down a bean stalk and killing a giant – how much more self esteem does Jack need than that?

Another objection is that I do not think such tales capture the essence of how stories work, which is through metaphor and multiple meanings. A single themed, 'Anne's parents divorce' story will not appeal to children for whom this is not an issue. At the same time, if it *is* an issue, such a story may be too close to home, too direct, and leave a child feeling vulnerable and exposed, something that should never happen in a school setting.

Alternatively, if you tell a story like *Snow White*, children for whom conflict and parental absence are very real issues may find great comfort in a story about a girl forced from her home who finds help and friendship outside her parents' world and at last finds a happy ending for herself. There is no need for children to admit, even to themselves, why the story is compelling for them and there is no need for anyone else to know, either. The king and step mother are metaphors for parents, the dwarves metaphors for friends, or helpers, or interests outside the home. Metaphors have multiple meanings themselves, so each aspect of a story, each character, can represent different things to different children. The story that can help a child going through parental divorce already exists, it is called *Snow White*, or *Hansel and Gretel*, or *Cinderella* - we don't need to write a rather artificial one to serve a single point.

To every argument there is an exception, of course. *Goodbye Mog* is a book about death and I think it's wonderful. However, it is first and foremost a lovely story by an excellent writer about a much loved character, and the 'point' does not get in the way of the story at all.

Stories - Space for Strengths

When I first encountered the work of Chris Peterson and Martin Seligman on character strengths and virtues, I was already using stories in school and linking them to the celebration of a cycle of festivals. I had written an entire book on stories and story telling and their potential to enhance the curriculum and build positive mental health. It seemed a natural extension to make a further link between the character strengths and the festivals and the stories so that teachers and children would focus on certain strengths at certain times of year and associate them with certain stories and visit and revisit them with each passing year.

In this way, children remember celebrating Advent by walking the Advent spiral and recall also that they were thinking about spirituality and hope and their importance in our lives. They will also remember hearing stories, the *Christmas Story* and others like *Cinderella*, that are told during the Advent festival. The stories will become associated in their minds with the strengths so that, at some level, when they hear *Cinderella* they will recall their work on hope. At the Performing Arts festival they might remember singing a solo at the special assembly and recall their teacher commenting on their courage. They will also come to associate the festival, again, with certain stories, for example, the story of *Caedmon and The First Poem,* as well as with certain strengths.

Linking the strengths to the stories seemed important but it is also important to remain true to how stories work. A story, a good, complex, centuries old story, is not 'about' any single thing. It has, as I have said before, many meanings and may mean different things to different people. At the same time, working with the stories and the strengths together, we realised that certain strengths shine out of the characters in a story and that the stories can, in this way, reinforce and affirm those strengths and show them in action.

It was a seven year old girl called Jade who really showed me the potential of stories as a way of indirectly reinforcing the character strengths. She was going to be singing a solo in the school's Performing Arts festival. I had told the children the true story of Caedmon, a shy young monk who overcame his fears to compose and sing what became known as the first poem in the English language. Jade said to her head teacher, 'I was really nervous, just like Caedmon, but I took a deep breath and was brave like him.' I did not and would not say to the children, I am going to tell you a story about courage or this story shows you how to be brave. The story itself made space for this child to find the courage inside the story, and to find support and affirmation for her own courage in turn.

I have gone on to make links between the character strengths and all the stories we use at the festivals – there are over 50 stories in all and this book contains a selection of them. They are indirect links and any story will show characters using a number of strengths. I would never say, 'this is a story about fairness'. But I might, if we had been thinking about the strength of fairness in class say, 'Could you see any fairness or unfairness in that story? Could you see other strengths, too?' That allows the children to continue to interpret stories for themselves and to find in them what they need to find.

In fact, as we worked with stories and strengths we realised that children find their own strengths reflected in the stories they hear. I did the Strengths Builder *Strengths Spotting* with a Year 3 group of seven year olds. I told them the story of *The Queen Bee* and asked what strengths they could see in the story. I could see courage and kindness. The group startled me by coming up with a good 11 different strengths most of which I had not noticed. I pushed the children to explain how they could see that strength or where it was in the story and their explanations and insights were excellent. I realised that they were very in tune with their own strengths and tended to notice them first in the story they had heard. In this way they felt affirmed in their use of that strength and noticed another way of using it they might not otherwise have thought of.

So, *The Three Little Pigs* is not a story 'about' curiosity, but the pigs show curiosity in going out into the world and trying out new experiences. They show other strengths too of course. *Little Red Riding Hood* is not a story 'about' prudence but it certainly has things to say about that particular strength, or the lack of it, as do many fairy tales.

When you are thinking and talking explicitly in class about the strengths linked to a festival, the children are more likely to notice those strengths for themselves in the stories they hear. It is infinitely more valuable for a child to make such links for themselves and to hear a story and notice a strength in it, than for you to say, 'This is a story about x.' The most explicit I would ever be, because I am a firm believer in the power of indirect learning, would be to say, 'We have been thinking about kindness, did anyone notice any kindness in that story? Or any unkindness? What else did you notice?' Again this is a question of balance and a place for you to use your own judgement. It is important not to close off the multiple meanings of stories or to impose our own, adult judgement, on a story. Children will always value our interpretations more than their own and you run the danger of undermining their confidence if your interpretation contradicts or is different from theirs – they will assume, 'I got it wrong. Mrs Eades must be right, it must mean this.' Mrs Eades is, of course, no more 'right' than they are.

At the same time if you want to use a story as a spring board to discuss a particular strength in an open ended way then that is appropriate too. For example, after a story like *The Elephant and His Mother*, you might ask, Which characters do you think showed kindness and how? This allows children to begin to explore their own ideas about the story and about what kindness looks like in practice. You might then ask the children whether they show this strength in similar or in different ways at school. The focus is on the children exploring their ideas in response to a story, rather than you telling them what the story means.

Story *Telling* – A Powerful Tool

I am not a purist and I am happy for children to hear or read stories or to watch them in film versions and listen to audio books. Reading to children, letting them hear excellent prose that might be beyond their independent reading level, is always very important. Stories are good for children, however they are delivered. However, there is something particularly powerful and nourishing about *oral* story telling.

When you read a book to children, you might edit a little and you certainly bring the story alive through your expression and dramatic reading. Essentially though, the words and the story are fixed on the page, written by a stranger at a point in the past, perhaps a far distant past. When you *tell* a story by contrast, however ancient the story, you are telling it anew, in the present, using your own words, your own awareness of the children sitting in front of you and the day you have spent together. All of that awareness, all of that insight, goes into the version of the story that you tell them. Story *telling*, in contrast to *reading* a story, is an active and demanding activity.

When you put the book down, there is nothing between you and the children. Actually, that is rather scary and is one reason why relatively few teachers *tell* stories, instead preferring to *read* them. You feel quite vulnerable without the book! 'What if I forget the story? What if they don't listen? What if they don't enjoy it?' are all fears that spring instantly to mind, however experienced the story teller, and you can't blame it on the book because the book is not there, only you.

On the plus side, it is quite the most invigorating and amazing experience to hold a group of children spell bound just with your words. It is one of the most fulfilling things I have ever done as a teacher. It is not only rewarding, it also teaches the teacher an immense amount. Story telling is a powerful course in professional development all by itself. It increases your awareness of group dynamics, you begin to understand how to use your voice to manage mood and behaviour, you learn how to use your body to communicate all by itself and how to use silence effectively.

Your ability to project yourself into the room by a look, by your stillness, just by your posture, will grow with each story you tell. You will discover that story telling is an amazingly effective tool for influencing the atmosphere of the classroom. You can use it to calm down a group of children or to stir them up, to comfort them or to challenge them, to add humour and enjoyment to difficult tired parts of the day, to close a session or a day in a deeply satisfying way.

Regular story telling sharpens your awareness of the effective use of language and rhythm and of the differences between spoken and written language. You are constantly exercising creativity as a story teller and the more you use a strength, the better it gets. You will become more creative, the more stories that you tell. All of these skills will increase your enjoyment of teaching and your effectiveness as a teacher.

Story telling is also profoundly satisfying for children. It is satisfying precisely because it is being done by a sensitive adult in the here and now. Adults 'tune in' to children's emotions. The more sensitive and thoughtful the adult, the more unspoken messages they pick up when they are with children. Stories are a great place to put those emotions and to convey on an unconscious level your understanding of the children you are with. You do not need to think about doing this; it will happen naturally whenever you tell the children a story. You put your awareness of their mood and their strengths and their backgrounds into the stories – because you love them. Since you are telling the story in the present you also add your sense of how the day has gone, for them and for you too. Children pick this up, again not consciously, and it helps them to feel understood, listened to, and cared for.

There is also something strange that happens when you tell a class full of children a story. It is a very intimate experience – again this is a reason that some of us find it uncomfortable. It is almost as if you are alone with each child. You are connecting with all of them very personally, through your words and especially through eye contact. The children are aware, though they wouldn't express it, that you are giving them something very precious that requires effort and courage on your part. You are giving them a unique version of a particular story. You are actually giving them a little piece of yourself. Story telling builds warmth and trust into a relationship as few other things can do. You will be remembered life long by these children as 'that wonderful teacher who told me those wonderful stories'.

Stories - Linking Strengths with the Curriculum

So far we don't have targets for teaching courage or kindness. However, we do have targets for speaking and listening, for literacy, for story telling itself, come to that. Why should a speaking and listening exercise not, at the same time, reinforce an important strength like kindness? It can, if the exercise involves a story that reflects that strength among others. Story telling can weave the strengths into the curriculum through the content of the stories and through the process of story telling.

In the UK, the national curriculum requires children to retell traditional stories. In Year 1, children are to retell stories using traditional story language and by Year 5 they are to have incorporated humour and repetition into their oral story telling skills. It is a bit hard on children to be expected to master a skill (and it is a skill) that their own teachers may be too nervous about trying it out. If children are to master the art of story telling, they need to see regular role models, adults who are confidently learning about oral story telling for themselves and who do it regularly. A school full of experienced adult and child story tellers would be a very confident and creative place to work.

All of the skills that you learn yourself from story telling the children can learn as well; a creative use of language, how to hold listeners by gesture and tone and expression, how to pace a story, how to project yourself while story telling. These skills will enhance children's literacy work, certainly. A firm grasp of oral story telling is an essential basis for writing because how can children possibly **write** a story if they cannot first **tell** a story? However, the skills imparted by story telling go much further than this. Story telling will help children learn how to tell anecdotes to people they meet and wish to become friends with, how to stand up in front of a group and hold their attention, how to behave confidently in social situations, how to become familiar with and express a range of emotions.

Story telling can also weave the strengths into the curriculum through the process of telling the story. Telling a story involves us in using a host of strengths. There is love of learning – we have to learn the story. There is persistence – learning and perfecting an oral story takes time. There is creativity – we adapt the story each time we tell it, finding slightly different words, painting a slightly different oral picture. There is friendship and empathy – the best story tellers are comfortable with themselves, their own emotions and the emotions in the story, as well as being very attentive to the emotions of their audience. Story tellers use leadership skills to gain and hold attention. They may use team-work if they are telling the story with a friend. They need hope and love because without these strengths, stories are barren. Humour helps! In fact, I am struggling to think of a strength that is **not** involved in the process of story telling. I include story telling as a Strengths Builder for each and every strength partly for that reason, and partly because the stories can reflect all the strengths as well.

Stories – A Medium for Values and Emotions

Children should hear a wide variety of stories from all over the world. Children in the Western world need to be exposed both to their own cultural heritage, conveyed through fairy tales and historical tales, and to plentiful stories from other cultures. It is then that we discover that what we have in common, the strengths behind the stories, outweigh our fascinating but potentially divisive differences. The strengths are universal and discovering that the story of *The Magic Brush*, from China, has a character who values honesty and so does the story of Rama and Sita and so does the story of George Washington, helps children to realise that humans have so much in common that can be used to unite and celebrate our shared heritage.

Sacred stories are important, too. All faiths use stories to hand on their beliefs and values to another generation and children benefit from hearing the stories of their own faith traditions and those of others. In fact sacred stories are a good introduction to another faith tradition because they invite the listener to make an emotional connection with the story, to 'enter' the story and feel just a little of what it must be like to see the world through different eyes.

Stories are also a powerful tool for developing emotional literacy and for helping children to understand emotions in themselves and others. Good stories contain the full range of human emotions, from joy and lifelong happiness through to despair, cruelty, shame and violent rage. It is not unusual for children to feel powerful emotions such as these. By telling stories that contain all of these feelings, we help children to realise that they are not alone with their often very powerful and sometimes conflicting emotions.

We all feel the full gamut of human emotions, including the less comfortable ones of hate, and fear, and cruelty. Most of us do not act on these feelings, and stories can reassure us that we are not 'strange' or 'bad' for feeling such things, while also being a safe place to put these emotions, what psychologists call a 'container'. Listening to a story that contains revenge, for example, allows us to indulge our own revengeful natures just a little, to find a release for an emotion that may be completely unacceptable to us, as well as to society in general.

Children who can 'project' their powerful aggressive or sad or fearful emotions into a range of stories are less likely to act them out. The story provides a way of feeling that emotion in a small, bearable dose, and for thinking about it too. Discussions which follow such stories can remain indirect, for children don't need to discuss their own emotions to learn about them, just the emotions of the characters in the story – a safe and indirect way of working with a sensitive area.

Stories – A Mood Booster for Everyone

Stories are enjoyable. Humans like telling stories and listening to stories. If you think you can't tell stories, listen to yourself in the staffroom at break time! Jokes are stories, the radio is full of stories, the television is story telling with actions! Stories boost mood – they can be used at the start of lessons to put pupils in a positive frame of mind, to **prepare** for learning. Especially (and I hope you do this) if they are *not* linked to the content of the lesson that follows but instead are just a gift, a good thing from the teacher to the pupils, just so they enjoy it. Used in such a way they would also be an excellent **repair** medium for those times when everyone, including you, has ended up being thoroughly horrid!

Story telling should also boost *your* mood which means you need to tell good stories and stories that you like. If you don't like one of the stories in this book, don't tell it. Or change is so that you do like it. Children learn, not so much from what we say, as from our enthusiasm. Do you remember the teachers who inspired you as a child? Can you remember the elements of what they taught you, or can you remember their passion, their humour and their enthusiasm? If you tell a story you feel uncomfortable with, your discomfort will communicate itself to the children and they will feel uncomfortable too, because emotions, like measles, are contagious. When I was a reception teacher, I refused to have a book in my book corner that I didn't like. If the children brought in 'Barbie Goes Shopping' I was willing to affirm their enjoyment of it but certainly wouldn't read it aloud to the class. I read books I found funny or enthralling, and the children were held by my enthusiasm. It didn't even matter, really, if they didn't understand the humour. The fact that *What a Mess* made Mrs Eades giggle out loud while reading it to them was something they found wonderful. It was their favourite book for a while, because it was one of mine!

I recently wrote a version of a Chinese story called *The Magic Paintbrush*. It is a good story, it fitted well with the themes of the festival we were thinking about and some of the children liked it a lot. I found I didn't really like it. I was going to leave it for others to tell, since life is too short to spend reading or telling stories you don't enjoy. However instead I totally rewrote it, made it simpler and more physical by adding Tai Chi moves and lots of going around the classroom drawing with magic paint brushes and now I'm happy with it. Find stories you like or change an existing one – you are allowed to change stories to suit yourself, that's how they work.

Stories - Building Habits of Positive Thought

The stories I tell are hopeful, optimistic tales. The twentieth century psychologist Bettelheim used this aspect of hopefulness, that is, a happy ending, as his definition of a true fairy tale. To his mind, the stories like *The Little Match Girl* were not fairy tales because they had sad endings and were insufficiently hopeful. Tell lots and lots of hopeful, optimistic stories. According to psychologists, there is something of an epidemic of depression in the Western world. More and more children, as well as adults, now suffer from mental illness at an earlier and earlier age. Telling optimistic, hopeful stories in which child figures conquer their adversaries will not cure depression but it can certainly do no harm in helping to build a picture of life that is more hopeful about the future.

Each thought we have creates a pathway in our brain. Constantly think gloomy, negative thoughts and you reinforce those mental pathways and make it more and more likely that your next thought will be gloomy, and the next and the next. Each positive thought we have creates a positive mental pathway and strengthens our capacity to think positively, to notice what is good, to avoid being an Eeyore thinker all the time. Hopeful, optimistic stories help to build positive habits of thought, speech and behaviour, just like the Strengths Builders.

Stories – Space for the Darker Side of Life

That does not mean, of course, that sad stories are not also helpful or good to tell. On the whole I use optimistic stories but there does need to be a balance. Sometimes we are sad, sometimes life is grim and children can find stories that contain sadness, even cruelty, strangely comforting. One of my favourite stories as a child was the Pied Piper. I loved the idea of the kingdom under the mountain, where all those children lived together with the mysterious Piper. I projected my own wishes and needs into the story and made of it what I needed to hear. It is not, by Bettelheim's definition, a fairy tale but it is a traditional European story, told in different versions placed in different towns, including one set on the Isle of Wight. It may be based on a real incident, and it is certainly a powerful tale and one that children enjoy and have a right to hear as part of their cultural heritage.

Optimistic stories are not without their challenges, either. Fairy tales, the definition of a hopeful story, frequently contain lots of violence, sadness, fear and death – and no fairies! I tell these stories and I put in the death and the violence and the fear, unlike some watered down modern versions. This is because, paradoxically, if you leave these difficult aspects of life out of the stories, you actually draw children's attention to them all the more and heighten their anxiety. You are saying, in effect, that sadness, violence, and death are too much for you, an adult, to cope with or even to talk about, let alone think about, face up to, and survive. I tell traditional stories which contain violence and death and children love them. I do not make them gory or emphasise the death and destruction – I just tell them quietly and matter of factly. These difficult issues are well addressed through stories and through stories they can become available for children to think about and to raise for discussion if they wish.

You have to be sensitive to your audience of course. When I told *Rumpelstiltskin* to a class of seven year olds, Rumpelstiltskin pulled his foot off before disappearing through the hole in the floor at the end of the story. 'Cool' as one little boy said! When I told the story to a group of younger nursery children I softened it a little, he stamped his foot and disappeared. When I told a traditional Orkney story, a variant on Rumpelstiltskin called *Peerie Fool*, to some Year 6 children, even I couldn't face the original level of blood and gore! However, I did tell the children what the original was, and the girls all went 'urghhh' and the boys all said, 'cool!' and told it in the original form with immense relish.

What Different Kinds of Story Telling are there?

Each story teller develops his or her own story telling style. Some story tellers use no gestures or different voices, making a sharp distinction between acting and story telling. Others dramatise part of the story, 'becoming' a character and moving between narrative and acting. Musicians might add music and song to a story. It is simple to take a well known tune and substitute different words and incorporate sung lines into the tale you are telling. A more visual artist would use props, or a painting, or a mask, or a puppet to bring a story to life. As with all other areas, follow your strengths.

I am a fairly quiet person and enjoy meditation. I started story telling using a quiet, meditative style that was influenced by a Montessori RE method called Godly Play. In Godly Play, sacred stories are told on a felt base using carved figures that represent the characters.

The stories are told quietly and while the figures are moved there is silence. The story teller makes no eye contact with the listeners, keeping their gaze on the figures. There is a separate set of props for each story.

I learned a great deal from Godly Play but I use very neutral props, like beads and shells and wooden bricks to retell both sacred and traditional stories. The props can tell any story and are not specific. I felt this exercised the children's imagination much more than having a dedicated 'pig' or 'prince' prop, as well as being much more cost effective for schools.

It is a very calming way of telling stories and an excellent way to begin story telling for adults and children alike. The props hold the attention of the audience, you can become comfortable with silence as you move the props slowly over the cloth, the visual and kinaesthetic dimensions appeal to different learning styles and, importantly, the props on the cloth help you to remember where you are in the story. Children love selecting and using props for their own story telling. They can exercise creative judgment without having to worry about whether they can draw or spell.

When you grow more confident as a story teller you can keep this quiet, calm method of story telling for when you want the children to become still and peaceful and to relax, perhaps at the end of the day or before a thinking skills session. There are other ways of telling stories that you can explore as you grow in confidence. See, for example, my earlier book, *Classroom Tales*, if you would like to explore this further.

Strengths Builder: Start story telling today
(*Use to build courage, creativity and persistence*)

If you've never told a story before, this is a good place to start. It's called The story of today. You do it with your class, obviously!

Start off with 'On a cold, dank (bright sunny) day in December (June) a group of children woke up, yawned and.......(a child supplies 'got out of bed') and then they.....and then they....' You keep going until you reach the present moment. Then, if they found that easy, reverse it and go backwards, starting with now and going on until they reach the point where they woke up.

Training Idea: A story telling session

Outline for staff the value of oral story telling and decide on favourite stories that each teacher and teaching assistant will learn to tell.

Working in pairs, use simple, neutral props on a simple cloth base to practice telling these stories. Keep the props few in number – I never use more than 10 and rarely that many. You don't need a prop for everything, you are just using them as visual prompts, a kind of 3D story board.

When staff feel competent they can use that particular story with their class and then with other classes too.

FIVE

Festivals and Celebrations

FESTIVALS AND CELEBRATIONS are the other ancient teaching technique besides story telling used within Celebrating Strengths not only to build positive habits of thought, speech and behaviour but to ensure that those habits endure, in individuals and in institutions. Every culture and every faith passes on the things it values through celebrations and festivals. Celebrating Strengths enables schools to do the same.

Festivals and Mental Health

When I studied children's mental health I became interested in how institutions, and especially schools, can foster positive mental health, flourishing and happiness in children. I had long been aware that anxiety is reduced by structure and predictability. I trained as a teacher of special needs and have worked with children with sensory and emotional additional needs; I am also very familiar with the challenges faced by children on the autistic spectrum. Whenever children have different needs from the majority of others, there is a high potential for anxiety. I have learned over the years a great deal about how to foster security and reduce stress in children. What is helpful for children with additional needs is helpful for all children, particularly at times of stress such as transitions.

In fact, all children face quite a degree of stress on a daily basis. There is an excellent and still unique book called *The Emotional Experience of Learning and Teaching*. It is written by child psychotherapists who studied educational settings and who highlight the anxieties and vulnerabilities we all experience in learning situations – whatever our age. The fears of not understanding, of failing, of being laughed at and exposed are quite universal and adults feel them as much as children.

In addition to this, children are changing all the time and are relatively helpless citizens in a world typically designed by adults for adults. Even the best of parents (and teachers) are sometimes bad tempered or under the weather and snappy. Children are reliant on us for their physical and emotional well-being. They must learn to deal with fallible but powerful adults. They must learn to manage the different environments and expectations of home and school. They must learn to separate from their parents and form relationships with other adults and with children. They must learn to manage the changes from baby to toddler, then to young childhood and middle childhood, through puberty and the upheaval of adolescence and on into independent adulthood. And they must pass exams and master fractions while they are doing this.

Even children whose home life is ideal have these challenges to face. Children from families who have experienced separation, divorce, bereavement or other stresses, have additional challenges to manage while they continue to master academic skills at school.

How, I wondered, could schools enhance what they already do to support children emotionally and become places where pupils – and staff too – can really flourish and grow?

A Cycle of Festivals

Several ideas came together to form the concept of building a cycle of festivals and celebrations unique to each school. One was a holiday in Spain, quite a few years ago now. We visited the town of Malaga and found, by chance, that we had arrived in the middle of a fiesta. Women, girls and tiny tots were wearing the most beautiful dresses I had ever seen, complete with hair combs and beads and shoes to match – they had taken immense effort and care over their wonderful appearance. Men were dressed with elegance and smartness – everyone seemed very happy and as strangers and tourists we too were made to feel welcome, a part of a festival we hadn't expected and the significance of which we did not understand. The celebrations lasted all day and well into the night! Why, I wondered, do we not have more celebrations in England? Everyone in the town seemed to be having such a good time!

The other idea formed from my experience both as a parent and from my Masters degree in psychoanalytic observation of families. I had begun to think very explicitly about what it is that makes happy families and healthy children and I noticed that good families have rituals, traditions. 'At Christmas, we always go and look at the crib in the middle of town.' 'On the last day of the school term my mum always cooked us a special tea.' 'On Fridays we always used to have pancakes for pudding.' The traditions are not actually fixed in stone – they evolve as the children grow and circumstances change but there are always fixed points, some continuity and explicit times of celebration and coming together – more than just Christmas and birthdays, important as these two celebrations are.

It seemed to me that in the past we had had, quite simply, more opportunities to celebrate. As still happens in some Catholic countries such as Spain, the feast days of the Church used to provide opportunities for communities to come together both for quiet reflection and noisy celebration. Learning to celebrate, learning to enjoy being with people, to enjoy song, dance, good food and drink in moderation would seem to be a skill that some societies have more than others and which provide the opportunities for sharing good times, thereby building closer bonds and stronger communities.

Celebration and Reflection

Celebration is all about focussing on what is good in life and, as has already been noted, we find more of what we focus on. Celebrate regularly and we will find more to celebrate, it really is as simple as that. In addition, celebration builds relationships in communities, between adults and children. Everyone doing the same thing at the same time gives us a common bond, a shared memory. Good relationships, as all teachers know, are at the heart of good teaching. Additional opportunities for adults and children in schools to relax and enjoy each other's company are important for building the good relationships that bind a learning community together.

Celebration also improves mood and happy children learn more effectively and happy teachers are better teachers. For all these reasons introducing more frequent opportunities to celebrate will improve the atmosphere of a school and build resilience and optimism in adults and children alike.

Reflection is also an important part of celebration. The celebrations of the church, the noisy fiestas, are preceded by times of quiet when the stories of the faith are told and retold, handed on to the next generation. These are the times when the community comes together to say what it is they believe in and value. Children, who also take part in such celebrations, are able to learn that these things are important, these are the values that adults hold and to which they can aspire.

It seems such a shame to me when adults say, of really our last and only festival, Christmas, 'It's for the children, really.' Well, it shouldn't be! Christmas is a celebration of hope, love and generosity. Hope, love and generosity should never be 'just for the children'. Christmas retells the Christian story of the incarnation – the amazing concept of the Creator of the universe becoming a human child and identifying with all the pain and suffering that are part of humanity. Why is that 'just for the children'? Whether you believe the story to be literally true, or not, it is a powerful myth and is at the heart of much of the art, literature and music that Western society has produced. Does that myth really have nothing to say to us as adults?

Festivals, times of reflection and celebration combined are a vital part of healthy communities and healthy lives. They are for all people, not just children. When you hold school festivals they should be for all members of the learning community to enjoy and benefit from, not just pupils and the odd teacher who has to be in the hall to keep order! Time to be quiet, time to feed our 'inner lives' as well as our minds, are important for all of us. The festivals are designed to provide this.

Seasonality

Another aspect of life that a cycle of festivals seeks to enhance is seasonality. The seasons of the year provided rhythm and structure for peoples' lives in the past, in a way that is lost in modern technological societies. We are farther from the earth and the source of our food and can eat strawberries in December – the joy of anticipation and the importance of harvest are experiences with which we may be unfamiliar. Today there are people advising us to return to more seasonal diets. This is largely for environmental reasons but I suspect that seasonality is also good for our mental health. There are three aspects to pleasure – anticipation, savouring the moment and remembering the good experience. When things are available all year round we miss out on the pleasure of anticipation. We may well fail to savour them as we might if we knew they would not be available again until next year. We may also not take the opportunity to look back and remember the pleasure of the strawberry glut in June!

Seasonal festivals, regular events in the school year, build on children's need for structure and predictability that reduce anxiety and help them to flourish. Enjoyable, special occasions that they know are going to occur each year will provide positive markers for the passing of time. They also help children to cope with the constant changes happening in themselves and perhaps with the less structured realities of life beyond school. They walk into school and they know what festival it is, when the next special event is coming, when they will hear their favourite story. The festivals give something to look forward to as each child will have its favourites, and afterwards they provide one of those important happy memories to look back on and return to.

The schools for which I designed the festivals were separate infant and junior schools. In each school I suggested that certain special responsibilities be given to the oldest children in the school – they would light the candles, help set out the hall for a special assembly, take part in the story telling. Younger children would know that when they got to be the oldest in the school, they too would have these responsibilities. You create traditions and you create roles to which people can aspire.

Introducing a cycle of festivals into schools has been a way of incorporating the benefits of seasonality and predictability, regular happy enjoyable celebrations, quiet reflection and the deliberate creation of happy memories into the school year. It benefits pupils, certainly. It is intended to benefit adults in the community just as much. Teachers need to relax and enjoy special events with children, to use their strengths in new ways in school, to have the time and opportunity to be quiet and reflective. We all need and benefit from celebration.

What do We Celebrate?

Perhaps the short answer to that question is, whatever you like! However, in this book I give an outline of a cycle of festivals which was worked out with a group of teachers in a school in Scunthorpe. It is only an outline. Develop it, change it, add and subtract from it until it is your cycle of festivals, right for you and for your community. You can take the principles behind the festivals and apply them in quite a different way – that is my expectation and my hope.

The festival we began with was Advent. Christmas is the only real festival left in the UK and, as a result, it carries a lot of expectations on its shoulders. This is *the* time that families come together, that communities gather in any meaningful way, that everyone is trying to be happy all at once – small wonder it is often very stressful. Would it be quite so stressful, I wondered, if we restored the ancient Christian tradition of Advent, the preparation period in the church in the run up to

Christmas, and had a slower, calmer and perhaps even more spiritual build up to Christmas?

This proved to be the case. The staff in the school where we celebrated Advent for the first time commented that it had been the most peaceful and most spiritual Christmas term they had ever had. Even the final afternoon, as the staff told the children special Christmas stories by the light of their class Christmas trees, was peaceful.

Then I looked at the concepts of beginnings and endings. These are important aspects of individual and community life. When I was studying anthropology as part of my first degree I become aware of the importance of ritual in marking transitions from one stage of life to another, while my background in group dynamics and children's mental health had opened up ideas about the anxieties – and potential – of beginnings and endings. Beginnings can be scary as well as exciting. Endings can be sad as well as bringing relief and new challenges. Having 'traditions' associated with beginnings and endings, 'things we always do at the start/end of term' can help to contain these emotions and to express them in positive ways.

So the next festivals we introduced were The Beginnings Festival and the Endings Festival.

Harvest was an obvious festival to include and develop. Most schools mark harvest in some way and it is a good time to focus on gratitude for the richness of our own lives and on a generous response to the large proportion of the world who have much less than us. Harvest festival is not a very old tradition, in fact. It started in the UK in Victorian times but some kind of thanksgiving is an ancient custom and one the schools wanted to build on.

The spring term, especially the first half in January and February can be gloomy and difficult. However, the Society for Storytelling has been running a National Story telling Week in the UK for about 10 years now and this seemed a good event to capitalise on. The staff decided to have a Performing Arts festival at this time of year, of which story telling would be one strand. It brightens up this time of year and brings a flash of enjoyment and colour into what can otherwise feel a fairly bleak period.

The staff then asked me to include Easter in the cycle. They felt that it was important to mark the two major Christian festivals. Easter can be perceived as challenging by teachers but it is a marvellous opportunity to focus on the strengths of love, kindness and friendship. We made links between this festival and the other explicitly religious festival of Christmas so that the children could perceive that they are indeed linked within the Christian faith.

The school wanted to mark each half term with a separate festival and the first half of the summer term did not have an obvious festival attached to it. We designed the Our Community Festival to allow us to focus not just on the school community but on the wider community, both local and global.

Other Faith Festivals

The two faith festivals we started with in Celebrating Strengths were Advent and Easter. These and other festivals contain elements from different faiths. There is a Buddhist story, *The Elephant and His Mother* that fits beautifully into the Easter theme of kindness, for example. The story of Rama and Sita is a key element of the Our Community festival, with its emphasis on honesty and integrity. Prayers from the Jewish and Muslim and Hindu faiths are used in different assemblies.

Initially, I did not design a faith festival from a faith other than Christianity for the simple reason that I am Christian. I did not feel I could, with integrity and authenticity, design a Hanukkah festival, for example. I would get some things right, perhaps, from reading and research, but I have not grown up with the stories and scents and traditions of Hanukkah. Because I am missing this, I cannot judge what is essential, and what is not, and how it might adapt for celebration in a school community by people of all faiths and none. I can do that for my own tradition, but not for somebody else's. It would not be authentic.

Now, working with a Hindu colleague, Reena Govindji it has been a pleasure to design assemblies based on the story of the journey of Rama and Sita and to broaden the possibilities of the Advent festival into a wider, Festival of Light. We have also incorporated elements of the thanksgiving ritual Raksha Bandhan into a Harvest or Thanksgiving Festival.

Similarly I would encourage people of other faiths to adapt the existing festivals and to design their own unique festivals as appropriate for their school community. The strengths that are linked to the festivals are universal and they represent what we have in common, while we celebrate our unique differences through the particular stories of each faith.

Reflection

I have already explored the importance of reflection as a part of celebration. There are Strengths Builders that are intended to build reflection into the school day and to cultivate the habit of taking a few moments to stop and look back at what has been good. *Reflections, WWW, Pearls* and *Good Bits/Bad Bits* are all examples of what I call reflective story telling, where you look back and select the positive events and either relate them aloud or doodle or draw them or just think about them. You could decide to do one of these activities during most days of a particular festival or incorporate them into the whole school assembly. I have done this successfully with *Pearls*, asking children to look back at the past few days and find a really good bit and then tell the person next to them about it. *Pearls* can make a particularly appropriate assembly in its own right toward the end of a term or a year. The Easter festival has six different reflections linked to the telling of the Easter story which happen in assemblies during the run up the holiday

There are also different kinds of meditation that you can explore with children. *Rain Stick Listening* is perhaps the simplest to start with but many activities can be meditative in that they are done slowly, calmly and with complete attention. *Colour Box* and *Creating a Story Space* build in meditation, quiet, focussed attention at the start of a session. The *Spiral* is a walking meditation. The whole retelling of the Easter story, *The Road to Jerusalem*, is a visual story meditation.

Stories

Festivals have always included stories. Religious festivals will involve the retelling of one or more faith stories. Local traditions will also have stories attached to them. On Orkney there is an incredible football game which is played each year on January 1st between the upper town and the lower town – the 'Uppies and the Doonies'. We are just summer visitors, but we have heard stories told about the Ba' and doubtless the post match celebrations will involve many traditional and possibly tall stories.

Stories are the vehicles that communities use to hand on what they value to the next generation, to remember people and events and beliefs that are important to us. All the festivals can have a variety of stories attached to them and examples are included in Part Three. You will find others you feel are appropriate to your festivals and your

school. They can be faith stories, they can be stories of historical characters who show the character strengths and virtues, they can be real
stories about your community, former pupils and teachers and their
courage and creativity and achievement.

Also linked with each festival are traditional tales. I tend not to
use these as much in assemblies, but there are exceptions. I have told
The Queen Bee in assembly, for example, and it seems appropriate to that
setting. Otherwise I use traditional tales more at the classroom level of
work. The links with the festival come through the strengths. Each
festival has strengths attached to it and the associated tales are those
that I feel show characters using one or more of the festival strengths.
The stories the children hear in the classroom thus reinforce the explicit
work being done on the strengths both there and in the whole school
assemblies. As the festivals come round each year they will come to
associate this story with this festival and these strengths. They will
anticipate hearing favourite stories told again, they will love hearing
them after a year's gap.

Some stories are likely to be told more often, not just at the relevant festivals and that is fine too. Do keep one or two just for the festival
though, so children and adults can experience the excitement of hearing
a story they haven't heard for a whole year – a simple pleasure but a
real one, just like getting the Christmas decorations out after they have
been in a cupboard for eleven months.

The Strengths

Each festival has certain strengths attached to it, on the basis of
strengths that appear to fit with the themes of the festival. At that
festival teachers in class will choose one of those strengths to focus on.
In assemblies, senior teachers will think, with pupils, about all of the

strengths associated with the festival, adapting Strengths Builders for the whole community and inviting children with a lot of those particular strengths to set an example and take the lead.

The links between the festivals and strengths evolved gradually with a fair amount of refinement and discussion. The final outline is a suggestion, no more. You may adapt and move strengths around to suit your own community. I have made changes as we have worked with the strengths in schools. However, I have kept much of Peterson and Seligman's terminology since we discovered that even very young children love learning the long words involved, and part of the work on the strength is talking about what, for example, persistence means. We can extend vocabulary at the same time as we work on the strengths.

Song and Dance

Whenever and wherever humans gather to celebrate, certain elements recur. Stories are one of those elements. Another is song and dance. Singing in a group is a very invigorating experience – scientists have recently begun to look carefully at singing since it is one activity that seems to improve well-being and happiness and to reduce stress. Studies have shown that choral singing increases immunity, reduces depression, improves cognitive function and releases endorphins, the 'feel good' chemicals. Choral singing also improves concentration and is dependent on teamwork and social awareness – a good choir member blends their voice with those around them and is constantly aware of their neighbours.

Singing elevates our spirits and is physically and mentally good for us and we don't have to be musicians to do it or, indeed, to lead it. Simple tunes can be sung by anyone.

Make links between the songs your children know and the festivals – there will be obvious ones that occur to you. If there are no obvious songs that link with the stories and strengths you are celebrating, then make up your own. I use well known tunes, often nursery rhymes and fit new words to them if there is no existing song to complement a story or a festival. You might have a 'festival song' that everyone learns and that is sung once a week throughout a festival. This can change year by year and the children themselves can make suggestions if you wish.

Dance is also a common element in celebrations though less so in our society now than it used to be. The simplest dance and perhaps the oldest is the walking circle dance. Make up simple dances to do with your class during a festival. Be brave and do a whole school dance if you wish.

I have done this in infant and junior schools as part of the Performing Arts Festival. I found a slow, beautiful folk tune and put simple steps to it. The children form large circles, together with all the adults present and at the end of the story of Caedmon, when the villagers in the story hold a dance to celebrate, the children and staff 'become' the villagers in the story and dance. In fact, the story of Caedmon also contains song since it is based on a hymn of praise written by a shy young monk that is considered to be the first poem in the English language. The children learn to sing a simple version of this song as well as to dance at the end and there is a great sense of completeness about the assembly where this story is told. It would be possible to adapt other stories, too, to include elements of song and dance. It is possible that song, story and dance were intertwined in this way in ancient times, and it is only our modern enthusiasm for neat categories and subjects that has divided them.

Colour, Food, Scent, Music.......

If you walk into an Anglican or Catholic church, you will know what 'season' of the church's calendar you are in because of the colours of the cloths around the church. I have used this idea in the festivals so there are colours associated with each one. The children will know, from the school environment, from the display in the hall perhaps, which festival they are celebrating. They may not even notice this consciously – but unconsciously the colours will help them to orientate themselves within the school year and add to their sense of security.

You might decide to hold a 'feast' of some kind at each festival – all celebrations, after all, involve food and drink. The preparation of each 'feast' might rest with different classes or year groups and you might decide to build in particular foods. We have 'traditional' foods at Christmas and Easter, of course, turkey and mince pies signal 'it is Christmas' to us as clearly as tinsel and carols. Chocolate and eggs do the same for Easter. You might develop this concept. At Harvest, for example, you might bake bread and use the bread to have a simple harvest meal together in class or as a school. At the beginning and end of each term you might have a special biscuit tin that comes out only on the first and last day of term. The summer is a good time of year to focus on fruit. Fruit picking, fruit salads, a fruity feast or picnic would all be possible traditions to establish – and healthy ones at that.

An important aspect of linking particular foods with certain festivals is the associated scents. When I think of Christmas, I think of the smell of pine needles and mince pies. When I think of Easter, I think of the earthy, hopeful smell of daffodils. Smells are intimately linked with memory, and a smell can bring back an experience in a way that nothing else can. Think about how you link wonderful scents to your festivals so that each time the children smell fresh bread, for example, they recall happy harvest celebrations in your school – not just when they are children, but throughout their lives.

Music is another essential ingredient of celebrations. I have linked certain pieces of music, as well as certain songs, to each festival. Again, children will come to associate different pieces of music – or different styles of music - with each festival. The associations will reinforce the memories of the strengths, the stories and the celebrations they enjoyed. Music can be used to set the mood and tone of each festival and can play at different times of the day, not just in assembly, but in and around the school. Having a cycle of music, as we have a cycle of stories, means the children will not become so familiar with a particular tune that they no longer really notice it. They will also enjoy hearing favourite songs again after a year's gap, just as we enjoy singing carols again for the first time.

In nature, there are patterns known as 'fractals, - the patterns of clouds, or the flames of the fire. Humans find fractals both soothing and rejuvenating. This is because fractal patterns are endlessly repetitive – they therefore calm us – but also intricate and complex and constantly changing and hence rejuvenating. The festivals you celebrate should be like this. They provide soothing, calming repetition – every year we walk the Advent spiral in the first week of December. They also provide different complex elements – the stories, the Strengths Builders, what you include in the whole school festival assemblies – that will constantly change and evolve. The festivals, like cloud patterns, or leaves on a tree, should both calm us and energise us.

What does a festival look like in detail? The final chapters in the book contain ideas and suggestions for each of seven festivals that form a basis for celebrating the school year. I have linked strengths that seem appropriate to each festival, and selected Strengths Builders that provide opportunities for building and using those strengths. I have selected stories that seem to echo those strengths. You may decide that a particular festival would be a good time to focus on other strengths and have favourite stories that you feel would fit well. Celebrating Strengths is not a blueprint, it is an outline that is designed for you to adapt to your own enthusiasm and strengths. It should evolve over time.

These festivals have worked well in schools and are intended as a starting point for your own creativity. Have fun!

Strengths Builder: Reflection
(Use to build self control, spirituality, gratitude and honesty)

Even if your school does not have festivals you can still build time for quiet reflection into your own day. Instead of spending every last minute in the morning rushing around completing more tasks, aim to be ready 2 minutes before the children come in.

Spend that final two minutes finding your own calm and your own stillness – look at a book of beautiful pictures, read a poem, look out of the window, listen to the sound of your breath. When the children come in, stop and smile at them and greet them one by one.

Try this for a few weeks and see how it affects your enjoyment of your teaching and how the children respond.

Training Idea: Celebrations

Talk to the staff about the importance of celebration and festivals. Then list what you already celebrate as a school, either weekly, termly or yearly. Can you think of additional ideas to expand your cycle of celebrations?

PART TWO

Three Levels

SIX

Celebrating Strengths in the Individual

Teachers First

CELEBRATING STRENGTHS is designed to help adults working in schools to enjoy their work more, to maximise the use of their strengths and to flourish. By flourishing I mean living as fully as possible professionally and personally while achieving your potential.

Flourishing is like measles - it is contagious. When we flourish, the students we work with are more likely to flourish and to achieve their own potential too. It is absolutely vital that you don't just *teach* the activities and ideas contained within Celebrating Strengths, you *practice* them for yourself.

The starting point for this is to be aware of your own strengths and to make a conscious effort to use them more often. You can do a strengths assessment online (e.g., the VIA-IS strengths assessment, **www.viastrengths.org**) which you can complete and receive a feedback report on your top strengths. The challenge then is to think about the different areas of your life in the light of those strengths. Do you use them at work, at home, in your leisure activities? Can you think of new ways to use them in all of these areas?

Research shows that consistent use of our strengths in new ways increases both happiness and a deeper sense of satisfaction with life, what might be called fulfilment. The more you can use your strengths in your work, the more effective you will be and the more fulfilled you will feel. If too much of your time is spent on activities that involve your relative areas of weakness, then you are likely to feel miserable and be considerably less effective than you might be otherwise. However long you spend on something that is a weakness, it will remain a relative area of weakness. That is not to say you should neglect or disown those parts of you, they are important too, but it is when we recognise and regularly use our strengths that we flourish.

Be open about your strengths with colleagues. It is not boastful to know and acknowledge what you are best at, because everyone has different strengths. A team that is balanced in its strengths and seeks to maximise people's opportunities to use them will be highly effective and happy as well.

Be open about your strengths with the students and children you work with. Comfortably accepting your strengths and being aware of areas that are less well developed sends a powerful message to children that it is alright not to be good at everything – and equally that it is alright to be good at some things. Some people struggle with both concepts. Acknowledging that certain strengths are not that well developed in you also opens up the possibility for you to pass responsibility for taking the lead in those particular strengths on to the class. The class is a team, like any other. When all the strengths are represented and used by that team it will flourish – we don't need to exercise all the strengths equally ourselves because a team mate will have in abundance the ones we have less of ourselves. There will be pupils who have strengths you don't particularly have – when that strength is needed, they can take the lead in exercising it. They will learn to take responsibility by doing this and to work for others as well as for themselves. The more aware you are of your own strengths, the more you can build awareness of strengths in the children, both their own strengths and one another's.

Display Your Strengths

A practical point to bear in mind is to display your strengths where you will see and therefore think about them as often as possible. This is called 'priming' and is explored more in Chapter 8 on the school environment. Surround yourself with references to your own strengths and you will inevitably find yourself musing about them and wondering how you might use them more often. And remember, we get more of what we focus on.

My strengths are displayed on my desk top. I look at them when I plan the activities for my day and try to make sure I am using at least some of them, some of the time – otherwise it is probably going to be a frustrating and unproductive day. I have also written them on the inside cover of my journal and my diary –that way I see them when I am away from my computer. I know what they are!

You could have them on display over your desk – why not let the children see that you value and use your strengths?

Listening for Strengths

When you become comfortable with the concept that you have strengths and raise your awareness of how often you use them, you can begin to notice and comment on the children's strengths in more explicit ways. Good teachers have always known the importance of appropriate and measured praise. Commenting on strengths is a development of that idea and one that will build self awareness and self esteem at the same time.

Having a list of the strengths up on the wall is a good idea because you will become familiar with what to look out for. When you see a child being persistent, brave, kind, hard working, curious, enthusiastic and so on, say so in so many words. Even the youngest children love to be told 'that was really persistent, you stuck at it and didn't give up, well done!' and they soon learn what 'persistence' means. You will find yourself observing children slightly differently as you wonder, 'what is their top strength?' and the more you look for strengths, the more you will find them, and the more they will occur, too. We get more of what we focus on: just by commenting regularly on the children's use of strengths, the more they will use them.

An important aspect of this particular kind of strengths spotting, is its role in building self esteem. If you praise a child for *achievement*, say for writing an excellent essay, they may then feel that to earn more praise they have to write another essay, equally good. They may also feel that if they drop below that high standard your regard for them will also drop. That creates insecurity and anxiety – it is the route many high achieving perfectionists have travelled, feeling they have to get an A* or a first, to be worthwhile.

If, conversely, you praise *effort*, rather than attainment, the child knows that you value them for their hard work, for their willingness to try, even if they don't succeed. Effort is within their control but achievement may not be. This builds a more robust and resilient learner and a more secure person, too. Commenting on strengths is another way of praising effort, you are commenting not on attainment, not on the A* but on the way it was undertaken, the humour, the imagination, the kindness shown to a partner. We can't all achieve A* all the time, but we can all use our strengths more and more. And children love to do so. They glow when you tell them they are being brave, or a good friend, or modest or wise, and will want to use their strengths even more.

If you are not sure what a child is particularly good at, careful listening and observation will show you. Alex Linley writes about listening for strengths and notes that when we speak about our strengths we are fluent, quite rapid in our speech, full of enthusiasm and the words themselves are positive 'I love doing x;' 'I really enjoyed y'. However, when we discuss our weaknesses we are hesitant, our voices are lower, our speech slower and more tentative and our vocabulary more negative with pauses and ums and ahs and sighs. It is easy to spot once you look for it.

The more you use the language of strengths in your day to day dealings with children and with adults, the more natural and instinctive it will become. You will find yourself picking up and reflecting back strengths almost without noticing you are doing it. Others will feel affirmed and better about themselves after talking with you without quite knowing why.

Children will not only appreciate and gain from your comments on their strengths, they will learn to comment on one another's strengths too. A new and powerful dynamic will have entered your classroom. Children who work in this kind of environment really do start to comment on each other's strengths – they internalise a way of thinking positively about themselves and others.

Building Strengths

Strengths can be built and developed. We may not all be naturally creative but we can all develop our creativity and enjoy doing so. The only strength, from Peterson and Seligman's list that I am not sure you can build is wisdom. It may come with age, though it doesn't always, and some children have it in spades but I am not sure if it can be deliberately cultivated. While wisdom can certainly be learned, many people would argue that it cannot be taught.

The other strengths not linked to the festivals are modesty and patience. These are important strengths too and you may wish to include them in particular festivals. Modesty is not included because young children need confidence and a good sense of self before true modesty can develop. Patience was added to the list later on, because it is so important for teachers. You may wish to develop your own Strengths Builders for these strengths.

Strengths Gym and Strengths Builders are all designed to encourage the use of and development of strengths. When used regularly they will encourage the development of the strengths in your classroom. Activities like *Philosophy* and *Story Telling* can be used as often as you like and can be done slightly differently at different times to build any of the strengths. You can explicitly decide with the children what you are going to focus on. They are all group activities.

You can also use Strengths Builders with individual children. They may be the same activities as those you use with the whole class but adapted for one child. An example would be the strength of courage. An individual Strengths Builder to allow children to explore this strength might say things like 'Speak to someone in the playground you have never spoken to before,' 'Put up your hand in class,' 'Speak up in a philosophy session if you disagree with someone,' 'Try something you know you find hard,' 'Try a new food,' or 'Be kind to the least popular person you know.' You and your pupils can think of other Strengths Builders to use like this.

You might display your Strengths Builders, both those for the whole group and those for individuals, on your strengths display and just have out the cards that relate to the strengths of this festival. You can then use the Strengths Builders, individually, in two, very distinct ways.

First, you can also use them with children who already have a lot of that strength as an opportunity to let them use their strength even more, in new ways and to really enjoy that aspect of school life. Second, you can also use them with children who you feel would benefit from more of that strength and encourage them to build courage or kindness or humour. Both uses are equally important.

Mood Boosters and Treasure Chests

Knowing how to improve your mood is a key part of emotional maturity and of becoming a flourishing individual. Everyone feels sad or angry at times, we are all human and I would not for a moment want to suggest that we try to eliminate these uncomfortable but essential emotions. However, uncomfortable emotions don't help us to learn or to be creative so knowing how to manage and modify those emotions is really helpful. Also, when you are going through stressful life events, being skilful at managing your emotions can help you to become more resilient. When my children lost their grandfather they grieved deeply, but they also knew that there were still things that made them feel more cheerful. So after a time of thinking, reflecting and crying, they would take a break from the pain and the sadness by watching a comedy, (we collect comedy DVDs), reading a favourite book, or playing their favourite instrument. The 'time off' would then refresh them and allow them to continue the important work of grieving for an amazing Grandpa.

You can begin to *notice the emotional after taste* of an activity or exercise, TV programme or book and, by making a note of it, build a personal Mood Booster.

Find a beautiful box, perhaps one with positive associations already. My box was given to me by a brave Polish woman called Marie who came to this country after losing most of her family in WWII and who lived next door to me as I was growing up. I look at it and think of her courage.

Into your Mood Booster you place the notes you make when you notice the activities that cheer you up or calm you down. The things you have done where you noticed, afterwards, that you felt really good. I cannot tell you what those activities will be, because they will be unique to you. Notice the emotional after taste of, for example, physical exercise of different kinds, reading different kinds of books, watching different kinds of TV, doing a craft activity, phoning a certain friend. The effects can be quite subtle so you need to become a skilled observer. Watching a drama on TV may leave you feeling tense but watching a comedy may cheer you up. Watching TV alone may feel sad, but watching with your family may feel much more energising. Phoning one friend may drain you, but another lift your spirits. Begin to notice and *note down* the things that energise and cheer you up. Write them on small cards and put them in your Mood Booster.

You are noting them down because we have a negativity bias in our brains – we are hard wired to notice more negatives than positives, so write down the things that leave you feeling positive. Then, when you are feeling low and want to change your mood, or when you need to do some learning or to be creative, look at your mood booster cards and select an activity you know is going to help. It is hard, when you are low, to recall positive feelings and to make creative decisions.

Having the Mood Booster to hand helps to make those decisions easier for you.

You can also build a Treasure Chest for yourself. Into this box you place objects and pictures which bring to mind positive things – pictures, cards from children, a holiday snap. Good memories, happy memories affect our mood in the present so having a collection of objects that evoke happy memories is a powerful tool for improving your mood. Have the Treasure Chest open and near you when you teach, to look at and make you smile at stressful moments. The Mood Booster will contain activities that make you feel better. The Treasure Chest, by contrast, is a store for happy memories. Both can be used to help you lift your mood when you feel the need.

When you are used to using a Mood Booster and a treasure chest for yourself and have become skilled at noticing the emotional after taste of events and at collecting happy memories, you can begin to encourage children to build individual mood boosters and treasure chests for themselves. These will be particularly valuable for children who find their emotions very powerful and sometimes overwhelming and who struggle with anger or anxiety or sadness. Giving children like this a tool that they can use for themselves is immensely empowering. Equally, emotional maturity is important for all children, so the happy, self controlled children will also benefit and enjoy a personal mood booster and treasure chest.

Body and Mind Connections

Adults and children alike benefit from knowing how the body affects the mind – and vice versa. If we slump on a chair or sprawl on the floor, our brains receive messages from our body that we are ready for sleep and react accordingly. If we hunch over and our face and whole body appears miserable, we are likely to start feeling low even if we didn't before. If we rush around like a whirlwind we will almost certainly feel agitated inside.

Conversely, if we are feeling low or tired we will usually slump. If we are feeling agitated we will tend to rush around like a whirlwind. How we feel emotionally, and how our bodies look and behave, are intimately linked.

You can take steps to use this connection positively. If your class is lethargic, we have always known that getting them to run around will energise them. What we have not paid as much attention to is the body's potential for calming them – and us – down.

If you are feeling tense, take a deep breath and let it out. Let your shoulders relax and begin to move and speak more slowly. It will have a calming effect not just on you but on the people around you. As a teacher you can use your own body to influence the mood and behaviour of your class. By calm, purposeful movement, slow and quiet speech, you will help the children calm themselves down and become more open and ready to learn. Story telling is a good vehicle for practising this technique, but do use it outside story telling contexts too – it is an important and very positive tool for building good relationships and a good group dynamic.

Letting children know, very explicitly, about this body/mind connection is important too. If they come in from a break feeling rushed and excited that is lovely but not necessarily good for quiet concentration. Encourage them to listen to their quiet breathing, or to do a very slow walk around the room, imaging their feet sinking slowly into sand as they do so. If they slump, let them know their brains will not work as well. If they feel nervous encourage them to put their shoulders back – their brains will think they are confident and their actual confidence will grow.

There are obvious links between this kind of body/mind awareness and the importance of regular exercise and a healthy diet. I happen
to think children and young people (and adults) should ideally start
every academic day with vigorous exercise because then their brains
would operate at an optimal level. Just walking briskly to school would
be a good start. If I am going to sit at my keyboard all day I go for an
early run first – I know that otherwise I am going to feel sluggish and
tired. If I need to be creative I run and then I meditate. If I am in schools
all day and haven't the time or energy to run, I go for a short brisk walk
in my lunch hour – just ten minutes in the fresh air gives me a clearer
brain and a more positive outlook in the afternoon.

Explanatory Style

How optimistic you are affects not only how you feel day to day
but also your success at work and in relationships, your health and
even how long you live. Optimists are less likely to suffer from depression than pessimists.

Children learn their explanatory style, which determines their
optimism levels, from the adults around them. You cannot do anything
about a child's home environment but you can make sure that their
classroom environment is an optimistic one.

Optimists explain difficult events in a certain way that contrasts
starkly with the explanations used by pessimists. If you are naturally
optimistic in your explanatory style, that is wonderful. If you are not, it
is something you can learn to do and which, with practice, will become
habitual. When bad things happen, pessimists explain events to themselves using two kinds of language. One kind is always/ everyone/
everything language. 'This always happens to me. Everybody hates me.
Everything is awful, all the time.' The other kind of language pessimists

use is nobody/ never/ nothing language. 'Nothing goes right for me. Nobody likes me. I never win at anything!' Both kinds of language are absolute. Think Eeyore, think Marvin the Paranoid Android, think of the poem, 'Nobody loves me, everybody hates me, going down the garden to eat worms.' That is classic pessimistic thinking – we all do it sometimes – if you do it often you are in danger of depression and probably miserable. Something goes wrong and the whole day is 'ruined.' You make a mistake and the lesson is 'awful.' A single bad event is allowed to colour everything around it.

Optimists suffer from the same number of bad events as pessimists but they react differently. They still feel low and they still get unhappy but the feelings don't last as long, because they are explaining the event to themselves very differently. 'The mistake was embarrassing but the rest of the lesson was fine. The bad event in the morning was horrid but the rest of the day was really good. John might not like me but Phoebe is my friend. I'm not brilliant at maths but my reading is really good. I failed this test – that's horrid – I'll work harder next time and do better.' The explanations are much more specific, much more temporary and actually much more realistic. This is not being Pollyanna, it is realistic optimism that says actually, not *everything* is awful. The outcome of optimism is persistence and ultimately, success. Pessimists give up, 'I'll never succeed.' Optimists keep going, 'I didn't succeed this time, I'll try again.'

When things go wrong in the classroom, listen to what you say in front of the class. Children notice. If you find yourself saying, 'Typical, this always happen' or 'Nothing ever goes right around here' try to pull yourself up and change the language you use. Make your language more realistic and more specific – 'This has gone wrong today' rather than 'Everything always goes wrong'. The more you consciously use realistic and specific explanations of bad events the more natural it will become. Gradually you will begin to naturally model realistic optimistic thinking for the children and young people you work with.

You can also explicitly teach optimistic thinking to children and young people using Strengths Builders like *Eeyore Thoughts* and *What Went Well? Eeyore Thoughts* is a game where you describe an imaginary bad event – and on purple thought bubbles write down the gloomiest thoughts anyone can think of. For example, the smart screen fails to work and an enjoyable activity can't be done. As a class, on a large purple thought bubble, write down the gloomiest thoughts anyone can think of. 'This always happens to us.' 'Someone hates us and has broken it deliberately!' 'This screen will never work again,' 'We will be bored for the rest of the day.' Use gloomy voices – it should paradoxically be a funny activity. Then, on a large green thought bubble, write down Tigger's replies. 'It worked yesterday and Mr Brown will mend it tonight.' 'Nobody hates us, computers go wrong sometimes;' 'We can listen to Mrs Barratt read us a book instead.'

You can use it to follow stories too. Tell any story and then point out that Eeyore would only notice the gloomy, scary, sad bits – I have a small Eeyore for this Strengths Builder. Ask children to draw the bits that Eeyore would notice. Then bring out Tigger, who would notice the cheerful, happy, hopeful bits – get them to draw them too. The children, of course, can notice both aspects of a story.

If you do this with a group you can also do it with individual children. Younger ones will respond to *Eeyore Thinking*, older ones can call it *'Explanatory Style Work'* – use it when they are feeling negative and pessimistic and work with them on the very worst explanations they can think of – using humour can be very effective – and then help them with some more realistic ones.

What Went Well is another way of encouraging optimistic thinking. It can be used for groups but it can also be used individually and children could have their own *WWW* folders to collect positive experiences, certificates, great pieces of work and to look at when they are feeling low, to boost their confidence. At the end of a day or lesson, encourage the children individually to find the most positive parts – even 'bad' days can have redeeming features but we have to make the effort to look for them because of our brain's natural negativity bias.

Use this technique yourself at the end of a day as a form of positive reflection and professional development. I have used it at staff meetings and training sessions. It is an effort because it is so much easier to recall what went wrong but like a muscle the ability grows with use and the more you look for positive aspects the more you will find. You get more of what you focus on.

Strengths Builder: Eeyore Thoughts
(*Use to build hope, self control, persistence and friendship*)

Begin to notice your personal Eeyore Thoughts and to label them as such. Try to find more optimistic ones to challenge or balance them. Personally I use the phrase 'Eeyore Thought' but you can use 'pessimistic' if you prefer.

Training Idea: Explanatory Style

Explain to staff the concept of explanatory style and its link to depression. As a group, think of some typical 'bad events' that happen in school and the kinds of pessimistic thoughts to which they may give rise. Then look at balancing these with more optimistic alternatives.

SEVEN

Celebrating Strengths in the Classroom

THE CLASSROOM is a microcosm of the school. The aspects of the whole school environment which will be explored in the next chapter are also true for the class room environment – the physical and the emotional environments need to be positive, challenging, safe places where failing is normal, laughter is frequent, and people expect the very best of one another, focussing naturally on strengths in themselves and others.

The Classroom Environment

Creating a great learning environment within your school can begin in your classroom. Start in your classroom and it will have a trickle up and trickle out effect – one flourishing classroom, one flour-ishing teacher, does have an effect on the whole school. Create a posi-tive classroom and you change the school, in small but palpable ways. Of course, it is better if all the classrooms are positive, but enabling one classroom to be positive is a start and a big step in the right direction.

Consider the lay out of your room and in so far as is possible (given furniture and architecture) make sure that it reflects your values. Do you value active learning? If so, movement should be facilitated and a variety of learning modes available. Do you value books? Make them prominent and attractive. Display excellence, whether in the children's work or from the works of leaders in the fields of art or maths or science – displays should inspire as well as reflect what is happening.

Strengths in the Classroom

If the whole school is using Celebrating Strengths then each festival will have certain strengths attached to it for you to focus on in your life with the children. A dedicated strengths display in the class-room can be most effective. In the colours of the festival and with the strengths of that festival prominently placed, it can then become a focus for thinking about the strengths. Children who have one of the festival strengths as a top strength can have their names on the display. How affirming will it be to see, 'Kieran is one of our leaders' or 'Jade's top strength is teamwork' written up for all to see? At some time in the year, as you cover a wide number of strengths, *all* of the children will see their own strengths on that display and their own names associated with them.

In addition, children you notice displaying the strengths of the festival in a particular way can have this fact acknowledged. 'We noticed Charis being particularly kind to Dan when he was upset yesterday – well done Charis'. Take photographs of children using their strengths and add those to the display. In this way, the display becomes an active, constantly changing reflection on the strengths of the festival.

If there are two or three strengths linked to each festival, don't attempt to focus on all of them in depth. Notice all of them and refer to them as often as you can, but choose the strength that appeals to you the most as the one that you will return to and actively try to build, through *Story Telling*, through *Philosophy* and through other dedicated Strengths Builders. If you choose the strength that appeals the most to you, it is likely to be the strength you are highest in and can be most enthusiastic about. So, for the Beginnings festival, the linked strengths are creativity, tolerance and love of learning. If creativity appeals to you the most, focus most upon that. It probably means that strength is higher for you than the others.

Strengths Gym and Strengths Builders

Set aside a little time in the week for Strengths Gym, a time to focus on the strengths of the festival and choose a game or activity to build one or more strengths. Some Strengths Builders, like those described below, can adapt to build any strength. When you use one of these, be explicit about the particular strength you are looking for – or ask the children which strength to focus on. This explicit discussion of the strengths with children is very important – we get more of what we focus on so focus, explicitly, on strengths. If you want to do some story telling during the Beginnings festival, tell the children you are focussing on creativity for example. If you do the same activity during the Our Community festival, you can focus on teamwork.

Other Strengths Builders are more specific and suit just one or two strengths. *Take the Lead*, which involves choosing a group activity and nominating one child as the 'leader', for example, very obviously gives opportunities for leadership. You will undoubtedly think of more of your own. Keep a 'Strengths Gym' file with a section for each strength; ask the children for their own ideas of how to use and build the strengths and let them choose favourites to do in an odd five minutes. If you brain storm with the children ways of building a particular strength, of using it more often, you could put their ideas up on the board and encourage them to sign their name on each one when they have used it.

As children move through the school different teachers will select different strengths from each festival to concentrate upon. At the following Beginnings festival the next year round, a teacher may focus upon love of learning or tolerance. It is up to senior management to ensure that all the strengths are brought to the children's attention through assemblies, through individual conversation and through the school environment, so that none are missed.

If your school is not using Celebrating Strengths and festivals, then make a strengths display for yourself and work through the 24 strengths over the year, drawing them to the children's attention, using stories that reflect them and thinking of Strengths Builders to help to focus on them. In everything you do, encourage the children to think about their own strengths.

At the start of ordinary class sessions you can also very explicitly state which strengths you are looking for. You could focus on team-work, or courage or creativity or honesty in a discussion, or open-mind-edness. Then you can ask the children to reflect for themselves at the end of the session on how they used a particular strength, how they might use it more and how they noticed their peers using it.

A focus on strengths would be an excellent way of greeting a new class. A discussion of what your top strengths are as a teacher – and of what their top strengths are as individuals and as a class - would be both positive and constructive. Acknowledging that there are areas which are **not** strengths for you gives you the opportunity to model self awareness and a realistic appraisal of your abilities – as well as to encourage the children to take the lead in those areas for themselves. Encouraging children to see one another in terms of strengths is a powerful way of building a group of individuals into a positive team who will work together for everybody's good.

Children who join a class part way through a year might complete a strengths assessment, either online or through a discussion with you that highlights their top strengths. A teacher I work with has used this method most effectively to integrate new comers into an existing class.

Flow in the Classroom

I described flow in Chapter 2 on positive psychology and education, that state when we are so absorbed in what we are doing that we fail to notice the passing of time. It is the time we function at our highest levels and are at our most creative. When teachers are in flow they are working to their full capacity. When children are in flow they are learning optimally. Creating a classroom that facilitates flow should be every teacher's aim.

For flow to occur there must be a balance between challenge and competence. If the challenge outstrips the competence too far anxiety results. This anxiety impedes, rather than facilitates learning. If competence outstrips challenge too much, and the task is too easy, we get bored. There are other elements which may be introduced alongside challenge and competence to help to achieve flow. One is play or, with older students, a playful attitude to learning. Young children playing enter a state of total absorption – they are certainly learning. There is challenge inherent in what they are doing, the challenge of making sense of the world, of the materials they are using, of the social relationships they are mimicking or engaged in. Another important element is choice or autonomy – they are in charge of the play process, they are choosing what to do and what to be, as well as choosing the level of challenge they are setting themselves as well. As we lose this sense of autonomy and do what we are told because we are told to do it, we achieve flow less and less. Reintroducing, as far as possible, elements of autonomy and choice into learning makes flow more achievable, more often.

Choices can be quite small but remain significant in their effect. One boy I worked with who was autistic typically found points of transition difficult and stressful. Introducing choice gave him more of a sense of being in control and therefore lowered his level of anxiety. The choices were not huge – for example, 'Do you want to finish that activity in three minutes or in four minutes' was typical of the choices he was given. But they were genuine choices. If he said 'four' I went back in four minutes. He found change much more manageable under these circumstances.

Introducing small choices whenever and wherever possible is crucial to enabling children and students to feel a sense of autonomy in their work and to achieve flow. Do you want to work with these bricks or those bricks? You need to do both these maths problems – I don't mind which order you work in, you decide. Choose who you work with, where you sit, what colour paper to use. Little choices can encourage the ability to make decisions and to take ownership of an activity – and help to achieve flow.

Another important part of achieving flow is the emotional state in which we begin an activity. Top athletes know they have to prepare mentally to enter what is often called 'the zone' but is really another term for flow. To function at their maximum capacity they need to be calm and focussed. Why are teachers and children any different? We arrive at a lesson rushed and flustered, they tear in from the playground or yard, squabbling and arguing and then we expect all of us to perform at full capacity and to be open for high level learning. It is unlikely to occur.

Consider taking a few moments to prepare for learning. To calm down, to focus, to think of something positive to boost mood or to use a Strengths Builder you know leaves everyone feeling cheerful. It need only take a few moments. If I am going to do something that requires a high level of listening from children, I usually begin with a few moments of 'rain stick listening', focussing explicitly on noticing the very last bead as it drops through my transparent rain stick. The children calm down immediately and focus. Any age of child or teenager can be taught to listen attentively as way of calming down, either to their own quiet breathing or to the most distant sound they can hear. Teenagers would enjoy a Buddhist prayer bell, you strike it once and listen to the echoes gradually fading away. They might use their imaginations to visualise their tensions floating away with the sound. What you are effectively doing is teaching children the basics of meditation as a way of encouraging flow and creativity.

Meditation

Meditation is perhaps an off-putting word for a technique and skill that is accessible to everyone, and which can be practiced by people of all ages and abilities in a wide variety of situations. It is not necessarily 'religious' - though it can be - and all religious traditions that I am aware of have some form of meditation as part of their spiritual practice. Meditation is also practiced by those with no religious beliefs. In essence, meditation is paying close attention to something, slowing down the chatter of the mind and becoming still, quiet and attentive. It helps us to become aware of the here and now when often we are lost in thoughts about the past or the future. It also helps us to become aware of our moods and less at their mercy – an important aspect of emotional literacy.

Meditation has been shown to have benefits for health and happiness and to improve mood. Since positive emotion and a calm inner state help us to learn more effectively it is a very useful tool for the classroom as well as an important life skill that children can use in other situations if they wish. I include different kinds of meditation as Strengths Builders for various strengths, but really it is such a good practice that it can be used to encourage any strength or even just incorporated into your general classroom routine.

It is entirely possible to teach children the basics of meditation and to introduce calming, quietening practices into the classroom that will improve mood and assist learning.

There are a variety of techniques for meditating. Some people repeat a word in their mind, slowly and thoughtfully. This is called a mantra. You might try this technique with the strengths you are working on. Ask the children, once they are relaxed and quiet, to choose one of the strengths of the festival you are celebrating and to repeat it in their head, slowly and thoughtfully. When their mind wonders, tell them, just bring it quietly back to the word.

The *Courage Meditation* is similar, though it uses a phrase rather than a single word. Quietly you say to children 'breath in your fears, breath out courage' and let them use their arms, drawing their hands to their chests as they breath in and pushing out their clenched brave fists as they breath out. This is actually the British sign language sign for courage. Repeat it a few times and start to use the phrase, 'Breath out courage' whenever you want to encourage them to be brave. If 'mantra' is an off putting word, call this *Word Meditation* and add it to your Strengths Gym.

I suspect that just as people have different learning styles, so different kinds of meditation will suit them. I have never found a mantra particularly helpful and prefer to listen to my breath as I breath out because I am an auditory learner. When I find myself thinking, I say 'thinking' and bring my attention back to the breath. This is a technique taught by a Buddhist writer called Pema Chodron. *Listen to Your Breath Meditation* is based on this, though I also invite children to 'see' their breath if they find that helpful or to 'feel' it going in and going out if they are kinaesthetic learners. It is important to say, 'Listen to your breath *which is so quiet only you can hear it*' otherwise you get a room full of loud panting!

Moving Meditations

Children, especially, may find moving meditations more helpful. The *Advent Spiral* is a moving meditation. Asking children to walk slowly, as slowly as they can, around the room without touching anyone and noticing the feel of their feet on the floor is a moving meditation.

Rain Stick Listening can be used as a moving meditation as children take turns to turn it over and watch the beads tumble and listen to the quiet sounds. A rainstick is simply a tube with beads or rice inside it that makes, as its name implies, the sound of falling rain. It is soothing to listen to. Rainsticks can be bought in music shops or, increasingly, in early learning shops. Mine is transparent so children can watch the coloured beads falling as well as listen to them. Using a rain stick, and asking the children to 'Listen as hard as you can. When the beads stop, listen to the silence' is also a form of listening meditation. It need only take a few seconds, a couple of minutes at most, but that may be all you need to quieten the children and improve their capacity for learning.

Alternatively, you can take a whole lesson and go for a *Looking or Listening Walk* to teach them to slow down and pay attention.

When you use props to tell a story slowly and quietly, with pauses for silence as you move the figures, you are using another kind of moving meditation. The children are watching and listening, though not moving themselves, but your slow movements and quiet speech will help them to become still and reflective. You may notice that you feel calmer after telling a story in this way.

Over the years I have built up a collection of props and cloths which I keep in a grandly entitled 'Story Chest' – an attractive basket with a lid that creaks as you open and close it dramatically. You can use such a chest in a classroom with all the children working in small groups of two or three to learn and tell a story. However the very best way I have found of using the chest, and of story telling in this way, is to go to a larger space, like a school hall and to literally *Create a Story Space*. This Strengths Builder is described in detail in Chapter 12 on performing arts.

You can really take any activity and turn it into a meditative, calming exercise. Unpacking the story chest to make the *Story Space* is an activity like this. The children are still, listening, waiting, paying attention and noticing in greater detail what they are doing and how. They are, in effect, meditating.

I do this with a box of stationery, too. Often after telling a story or following a discussion, I want the children to follow up by drawing or doodling in some way, so that ideas and images can settle and work in them. One way of encouraging them to be creative and reflective is to take a meditative approach to unpacking the stationery box. It is a beautiful wooden box, which opens to reveal a spectrum of coloured pens, pencils and pastels. It is aesthetically pleasing and a joy to look at – which is important as it draws the children's attention more effectively than a tatty pencil case. I place the box – I call it the 'colour box' - in the middle of a circle if the children are on the floor, or on a table if there is really no room for a circle. Then I point to one child who gets up and selects two things from the box. As that child comes back I point to the next child and so on. In thoughtful silence, the children come up and make their choices, while the others look on, waiting. It is a quiet, thoughtful, calming interlude. It takes time and you would not always get pens out in this way. If you did, the effect would be lost, and it is also so slow that you would never get anything done. However, done occasionally, it can be an effective form of meditation, teaching patience, attention and the importance of quiet, calm movement in managing your own emotions.

Other Calming Meditations

You can do most things and make them meditations. Try making a cup of tea with complete attention. Notice the shape of the tea pot and the cup. Listen to the sound the kettle makes as it comes to the boil. Notice the texture of the tea or the shape and colour of the tea bag. Drink with attention, think of all the people and processes that have enabled you to drink this cup of tea – say a quiet thank you to all of them. That is meditation.

Visualisation is another kind of meditation and one that can be very effective with children. You can start the day by taking a minute to invite them to breathe quietly, to relax and to see themselves having a really good day. Ask them to make a film in their heads – a really colourful film – and to notice that the 'them' in the film is looking happy, confident and creative and is enjoying getting things done. Ask them to sit straight, to put their shoulders back and, with their eyes closed, to grin as widely as they can. They can then open their eyes and begin a really good day.

These are simple techniques but they can be very effective. Smiling really does make you feel better. Putting your shoulders back also has a positive emotional effect because our bodies and our feelings are intimately linked.

Pearls is also a kind of visualisation, though this time using happy memories rather than looking forward. Happy memories, when we bring them to mind vividly, have a positive emotional effect in the present. Remember a happy day and you can experience the enjoyment all over again. ***Good memories are a storehouse of happiness.***

Story Telling Meditations are another kind of visualisation. Some of the stories from the Easter festival can be done in this way. You invite the children to relax, to close their eyes, to breathe quietly. You might put quiet music on in the background – it helps some children to concentrate, though not all. Then you tell the story of, for example, Jesus entering Jerusalem on a donkey, inviting the children to put themselves into the story, to make a vivid, colourful film of it in their heads, to see themselves in the film, then to step inside that world and look around them. They can talk to the characters and listen for what they reply.

This kind of visual meditation, based on a story from the bible, is also a kind of prayer called Ignatian prayer. It is an ancient tradition within the Christian church and children enjoy it very much. They can follow up the story by drawing or writing or retelling it using props either alone on in a pair. The follow up needs to be unstructured so that they can mull over the meaning of the story for themselves.

Savouring is yet another kind of meditation. Using chocolate, or a piece of bread or fruit, the children learn to slow down and eat with full attention. It is calming and fun, and they are learning and becoming more available to learn without really noticing. Following activities such as these, the children are going to be much more ready to learn after 30 seconds of quiet concentration, than in a rushed state having piled in from the playground or canteen.

Story Telling in the Classroom

A classroom where teacher and pupils tell stories regularly is going to be a positive, creative and enthusiastic place – it can't be anything else. Tell stories regularly, learn to be a story teller and encourage the children to do the same. Learn one or two to start with and tell them often – children enjoy repetition, look at how often they will watch a favourite film. Fill odd five minutes with stories.

When telling traditional tales or myths, I like to use simple objects like stones and glass beads on a cloth base. The objects can represent all or some characters in a story while the cloth becomes the imaginative 'world' of the story. I move the objects slowly, with frequent pauses in between my words and I talk quite slowly too. This is a very calming way to tell stories – the slow movements and measured speech have a very soothing effect on listeners and on the story teller too. The neutral props provide a visual and kinaesthetic element to the story telling, while leaving maximum room for the listeners to use their imaginations. Children can learn to tell stories in this manner for themselves and it can be used for any kind of story, including traditional folk stories, fairy tales, myths, legends, and sacred stories from different faiths.

Philosophy

Philosophy with children is an excellent positive tool to use in the classroom regularly. It is not new - Mathew Lipman was writing about it over 20 years ago - but it is now growing in popularity and rightly so. It is challenging for teachers because it asks them to take a back seat and to facilitate rather than actively 'teach.' Learning to keep quiet in a discussion and allow the children to pursue their own reasoning without imposing my opinions or wider knowledge is something I have found extremely difficult to do at times. However, philosophy is worth pursuing if you wish to build a positive classroom because it creates such a powerful dynamic in the classroom and allows children to exercise autonomy, to learn to ask questions for themselves and to engage with ideas and with one another in confident and appropriate ways.

Philosophy is a versatile tool that can be used to explore any of the strengths. It can also be used as a way of using many of the strengths, so I include it as one of my Strengths Builders. You can use a philosophy session to discuss 'What is love? What is courage? What is forgiveness?' And you can use philosophy sessions to provide opportunities to use strengths like courage and creativity. It takes courage to disagree with a large group or a popular idea. It takes creativity to think of an idea of which no one else has yet thought. You can reflect, at an end of a session, on how individuals, and the group as a whole, used their strengths.

You can build philosophy into any subject and use different starting points. A common approach is to start with a stimulus like a story or a poem, a painting or even a piece of music and then to ask the children to think of their own questions which they would like to discuss. When I do this I find at first that I have to draw a distinction between what I call 'thinking questions' and 'factual questions' – the former are those that will lead to more complex discussion. Questions such as 'Why did this character do that?' 'Is the story true?' 'What would have happened if....' tend to lead to more fruitful discussions than 'What colour were his shoes?' I don't have to labour the point, however, as children soon learn to pose these deeper kind of questions for themselves.

Then the children choose with which question to start. I encourage them not only to reply to the previous speaker but to make sure they speak *to* them, so that social skills are honed in the process. Not, 'I agree with John,' but 'I agree with *you* John'. Learning that they can agree and disagree with one another can be a liberating discovery for children and one they can carry over to the playground and beyond.

Class Mood Boosters and Treasure Chests

In Chapter 6 I described how you could create for yourself a Mood Booster and a Treasure Chest and help individual children to do the same. You can also build class *Mood Boosters* and *Treasure Chests*. Into the *class mood booster* goes the title of all the books they love, the songs they like singing, the Strengths Builders they enjoy the most, the stories they ask for again and again. You build this resource throughout the year as you notice what they particularly enjoy, what calms them down, what cheers them up. You invite them to choose one for the start of a lesson, to **prepare** for learning or after a bad lesson, to **repair** everybody's mood.

Or you choose one yourself. Never be afraid to include *your* favourite activities or stories or games in the class *Mood Booster*. Why should *they* be the only ones to choose what to do? Let them know that you are going to retell a particular story in an odd five minutes, not because it fits the curriculum plan but because, horror of horrors, you want to! They will enjoy it because *you* enjoy it – and they will learn an important lesson about enthusiasm and love of learning. In an ideal world you would only do things you love in a classroom because we teach first and foremost by our love and enthusiasm for a subject and we cannot fake an enthusiasm we do not feel. That is not always possible because we do not live in an ideal world. However, where you do have real enthusiasms, let them show and indulge them as often as you can. Good teachers always have.

The class Treasure Chest might be a photo album of snaps of trips and lovely pieces of work and visitors to school, of festivals and celebrations. It is something to store the class's happy memories in.

The important insight that positive mood enhances learning can be reflected practically in how we manage our classroom. We can turn to either the *Mood Booster* or the *Treasure Chest* as a way to start lessons or days so that these important moments become positive, building a sense that learning is enjoyable and worthwhile.

The end of a day or a lesson should ideally be positive too. How you look back on an event is determined by the most intense part of the experience and how it felt just before it ended. This means that an overall good day that had a really bad argument in it and where you ran out of milk and couldn't have your hot chocolate at bed time will be rated a bad day. Conversely, a difficult day that had a really funny event part way through and a peaceful evening, will feel overall like a good day. Our memories are not that accurate.

If you can build into each day or each lesson one really fun experience and a positive end, pupils looking back over the day will rate it positively even if the rest of the day was more mixed. That will encourage them to anticipate a good day tomorrow and overall to rate 'education' as a positive experience, and hence one which they are more likely to continue with throughout their lives. The *Mood Booster* and the *Treasure Chest* provide a practical tool for doing this.

Positive endings can also be encouraged by activities such as *WWW* or What Went Well? This can be done in different ways. One is to do a kind of oral story telling where each child provides you with one positive event in the day and you weave all of them into an oral story, *The Day of Class 6B,* for example. Or mind map the positive events of the day and leave the mind map up to look at as soon as you come to school the next day – the positive ending then becomes the positive beginning.

Pearls is another Strengths Builder to use as a positive end. Everyone needs to think of one 'pearl' from the day, a kind word, a success, a cake at lunch time, a moment's laughter, that they will take away with them as they go home. They need to remember that moment, the sights, the sounds, the feelings of it, to relive it all over again. Children can have an actual 'pearl' to keep in their desk, a glass bead that they imprint with happy memories. They can be given out in September as part of the Beginnings Festival to collect memories throughout the year – then taken home in July and kept forever. Younger ones I tell to hold the pearl in their hand and blow on it three times – the memory is now 'inside the magic memory pearl'! Taking a moment at the end of the day to recall and savour its happiest moment will increase positive emotion in the present and provide a happy memory to go back to in the future.

You don't have to do such activities every day but you do need to persist with them to have an effect. Change requires persistence and effort, and until it has become a positive habit, something you all do almost without noticing.

Strengths Builder: Start a personal mood booster
(Use to build hope, persistence, self control, spirituality, forgiveness, prudence)

Begin to notice what you are doing when you feel really good – either at the time or just after the activity. Write down these activities and collect them in a beautiful box as a personal resource. Learn to notice the 'emotional aftertaste' of activities and events.

Training Idea:

Explain the effects of mood on learning, how a cheerful mood improves memory, verbal fluency, lateral thinking and creativity.

Invite colleagues to think of activities that you might do to improve mood

- At the start of lessons
- At the start of staff meetings

EIGHT

Celebrating Strengths in the Wider School

CELEBRATING STRENGTHS operates at three different levels: the individual level, whether that is an individual staff member or pupil, the classroom or class group level and at the whole school level. Ideally all three levels will work together, and this will inevitably be the most effective way to use Celebrating Strengths. However, we do not live in an ideal world and it may not be possible to introduce all the levels immediately. Therefore they are designed to be used independently as well and will still have a positive effect – small changes can make a big difference.

The Strengths in the Wider School

Just as it is useful to have the strengths on display in the class-room, so they can also be on display around the school. We can 'prime' our environment with positive images and words because what we look at every day and what we habitually think about affects us, either positively or negatively.

In a Harvard lecture on positive psychology, Tal Ben Shahar quotes a fascinating study that illustrates this point. A psychologist gave two cognitive tests to a group of students. In between the tests he asked them to think of synonyms for words like 'elderly, wrinkle, old,' and then he retested them. As they walked away from the laboratory, he timed the speed with which they walked a measured distance away from the tests. After thinking of words associated with old age, the students performed worse on the cognitive tests, and their movements had actually slowed down. Conversely, when he repeated the test, but asked the students to think of synonyms for words like 'succeed, thrive, energetic,' then the students performed better on the second test, and their movements speeded up. What we focus on, the words we hear and see around us, and what think about, has a real and measurable effect on our performance.

Filling our physical environment with positive words and images is called 'priming.' What your school looks like is an obvious way of conveying meaning and values both to the members of the community and to visitors. When you first enter the school what do you see? Is there a message about the purpose of the school? I sometimes wonder if children realise why they are in school at all, other than that they 'have to be there because the government says so'. What is the purpose of the school and is it clearly spelled out in words that literate children can read and pre-literate children have read to them regularly? Are the core values and beliefs of the school on display in a prominent place?

Good businesses have visible mission statements for a good reason – what we read regularly does have an effect on our attitude. Our environment affects us, positively or negatively.

The schools I have been working with use strengths in their displays. The children see the strengths associated with the current festival on the wall in the hall and in the classroom. Displays will interweave these and other strengths into their language. 'We have used our creativity and persistence to produce these water colour paintings'

'Our school council have been thinking of ways we can encourage kindness' 'The story of Easter reminds us of love and forgiveness'. There are also, in some of the schools, inspirational quotations on the walls, again linked with the strengths of the festival. Just walking around the school, adults and children are reminded of what is important, what the school believes in and aspires to.

Having uplifting images, great art, on the walls also affects us. Keeping the classroom and communal areas tidy, putting effort into creating a beautiful, peaceful environment speaks volumes about our care for the children – and will also, as studies have shown, affect their capacity to learn.

At the whole school level, Celebrating Strengths can also inform the school's mission statement and overall ethos. Does the school have a strengths based mission statement and are all members of the community aware of it? Do staff members spend time considering the strengths of their team and do senior management make use of a strengths based approach to managing and coaching less senior colleagues? Do senior management take care of their own well-being and foster their own strengths?

We can also fill the emotional environment of the school with the strengths. When you are familiar with the language of the strengths you will notice them in children more and more and the school will become more and more positive – even without you consciously trying to achieve this. The children will pick up the language of the strengths themselves and will follow your example – their own relationships will become more positive and affirming.

The Strengths in Assemblies

Assemblies have a vital role to play in Celebrating Strengths and are a highly valuable tool for anyone who wants to build community. Occasionally someone will argue that assemblies should be abolished and that they are inappropriate in a multicultural and largely secular society. I could not disagree more, though I understand why this is said. Far from abolishing assemblies, I regard them as the single most important event in the school day – an essential community building tool, a peaceful oasis for reflection for every member of the school community. Assembly is when the values of a school are reinforced and communicated; it is when achievements are celebrated and sadness and hurts acknowledged; it is where children learn that stillness can be soothing and liberating; and where the stories of many faiths can be told again and listened to for inspiration in how to live well. Assemblies are a gift to the educator. Used well, they can transform the atmosphere of a school and set the tone for the day.

They are also a perfect opportunity for celebrating the strengths. You can talk about them, ask children to share how they have used them, read and tell stories that echo them. I use a sign language dictionary to find signs for all the strengths and teach them to the children at each festival – they remember them from year to year and signs can be used most effectively as visual prompts. Making the sign for 'kind' for example, hand on heart then moving outwards in a thumbs up gesture, is a more effective reminder than, 'Don't do that George, it's not kind to Abigail'!

Assemblies can be simple but beautiful. Carrying a lighted candle to the centre of the hall to mark a quiet beginning. Having a display that beautifully reflects the colours and strengths of the festival. Spending time in silence remembering a pearl from yesterday or a hope for today. Telling a story simply, with actions or signs the children can join in. All these are ways of making assemblies an oasis of quiet in the school day.

Using simple prayers or affirmations from around the world and putting signs to these can be very effective. Say a prayer or affirmation and put signs to it, then 'say' it again just with your hands. A perfect ending to an assembly and a safe introduction to silence for children.

Silence is essential for reflective assemblies and it is something you create, not just an absence of noise. Slow, deliberate actions can be used to build silence. I light a candle before the assembly begins – I used to light them at the start of the assembly but when matches go out it causes giggles which wrecks the atmosphere I am trying to create - so now the candles are lit beforehand. I am ready, waiting, already calm and quiet before the children enter the hall. I will have taken a minute or two to find my own peaceful stillness, which is there underneath the nervousness I always feel at the start of a school day.

I smile at the children as they enter and sit down, already they will be influenced by my stillness. When they are all seated and the music is turned down I stand and deliberately, slowly, move to the side, pick up the candle and return to the centre of the room, or to the table at the front and place the candle in full view to signal that the assembly has begun. I have created silence. Children can be taught to start the assembly for you in the same way, moving slowly to place a candle in a prominent place.

Story Telling at a Whole School Level

The stories that are told to the whole school become part of your shared knowledge, shared memories and a powerful way of reinforcing shared values and a respect for all the strengths. A story conveys values and strengths and beliefs to children without patronising them or forcing them to conform. Stories suggest and invite a response – we can take them or leave them, together with the meanings they may contain.

I would encourage you, once more, to put books down and *tell* stories if you can, rather than *read* them. The story immediately becomes more powerful, more direct, more suited to its listeners because the story teller, unlike the story reader, selects their words in response to their listeners. If the listeners become restless the story teller knows that something is amiss and can respond immediately, with fewer words, more expression, more silence, more inclusion.

Story telling to a large group is not easy but it is perfectly possible with awareness of some simple techniques. I know of one professional story teller who refused to tell stories in the hall to more than 30 people – that is a shame. Yes, it is a challenge to tell a story in assembly but it is also a very effective thing to do. Children love it and so do adults.

Stories need to be simple and short for use in a large group. Mine never last more than 5 minutes and often less. Never be afraid of brevity! And never start unless the silence in the hall is complete. You can use objects to create silence and you can use your body. When the *Road to Bethlehem* and *Road to Jerusalem* stories are to be told in assembly, pebbles are used to build the road at the start of the story, slowly, one by one, placed in a line across the hall, the leader standing up each time, going to get another pebble and placing it gently, ever reverently, onto the floor. You will want to rush, you will feel silly, you will think they can't possibly sit still for so long. Notice all these thoughts – I get them all the time – but don't act on them. Keep your movements slow, graceful, deliberate and pay attention to the pebbles not the children. Their gaze will follow yours and they will look closely at the pebbles if you do. I guarantee the children will be very quiet and totally absorbed by what you are doing by the time you have finished! Then, the story starts.........

Include the children where possible. When I first began telling stories in assembly I used stories such as *Benno and the Beasts* where the children can supply animal noises as the story progresses. It was immense fun but the children grew very excited and, I noticed, really stopped listening to the rest of the story. It was not the quiet, listening atmosphere I wanted. So I began to ask them to use gesture instead of sounds.

Sometimes I would teach them a British Sign Language sign for a word that I would repeat throughout the story and they could help me to tell the story, I explained, by making that sign whenever they heard the word. So, for example, I would tell the Native American Indian story of the *Spirit of the Corn* and the people who *forgot* to say thank you. Each time I said the word *forgot* the children would make the BSL sign, which is literally like taking something out of your head with your fingers. Or, when I tell the story of St Werburga, *One of my Geese is Missing*, the children listen out for the phrase 'Great long snake like necks' and use their hands as a goose's head, weaving through the air.

This method works very well indeed for helping children to focus on the story, to really enter into and take part in it, but quietly, thoughtfully and with attention.

I often end stories with creative silence, by asking everyone to join in a silent, signed prayer that fits with the theme of the story. It is a simple but powerful way to close. I never explain what the story is about! That's not how stories are meant to work. I leave them to sink into the silence instead.

The Festivals at the Whole School Level

Strengths Builders can be adapted to work at a whole school level. If every class in the school does the same Strengths Builder it becomes a whole school event and celebration. *Story Telling* can become a story telling day when staff and teaching assistants (and caretakers and dinner ladies) go from classroom to classroom telling their favourite stories. The *Advent Spiral* is a Strengths Builder – but if the whole school do it, class by class, it becomes a shared memory, a community building activity. You might choose as a class to use *Hospitality*, from the Strengths Builders for teamwork. If every class in the school does the same you might have a week of writing invitations, baking cakes, hosting parties – a Hospitality week when friends and neighbours are invited into school – do it two years in succession and you have invented a school tradition.

The appearance of the school can also follow and enhance the sense of rhythm created by the festival cycle. If you associate particular colours with each festival and have key displays round the school that always echo those colours, just seeing those colours on a display will remind the children for example, that this is early summer and we are thinking about 'Our Community.'

It will also, very importantly, remind them subtly of the strengths you always focus on during that festival - in my suggested outline these are leadership, teamwork and honesty. You are quite deliberately creating unconscious positive links for the children to increase their sense of security and their positive feelings towards school. You are reinforcing important values just by the colour of the drape in the entrance hall.

You might have a display of all the festivals in the year to help the children orientate themselves in time, to see where they are now and when their favourite festival will come round again. One school has a festival wheel that has an arrow pointing to *this* festival and pictures from them all displayed at the right place. This helps children enjoy the pleasure of looking back at what they did and look forward to the next festival. It also builds a feeling of security.

Sensory Impressions Around the School

Smell is strongly associated with memory and with emotion. The scent of coal tar soap makes me nervous. It brings back less than happy memories of infant school. On the other hand I love the smell of pipe tobacco – my father smoked a pipe. Smell seems to by pass our rational adult self and to give us a powerful emotional jolt. There are physiological reasons for this – the part of the brain that deals with smell is directly linked to the amygdala and the hippocampus, which deal with emotions and memory respectively. This explains why memories evoked by smell are often very emotional ones – you will have had similar experiences yourself. If you want to create happy memories for children – and that is a central theme of Celebrating Strengths – pay careful attention to the scents associated with each festival. Just as the scent of pine needles, for many people, brings Christmas strongly to mind, you want deliberately to make positive links between wonderful smells and the festivals you are creating.

Harvest is a good time to bake bread, for example. When telling *The Story of Bread* in assembly I take in a freshly baked loaf so that its scent wafts through the hall. Baking bread would be even better. You probably do this at some time in the school year anyway, so consider linking this activity, each year, with the harvest festival and with stories about food and the strengths you focus on during harvest. By doing so, you will create happy, positive memories for the children. It would be no bad thing to have a generation of children who associate the smell of bread with thoughts of gratitude, generosity and fairness!

Be creative in making olfactory links. Christmas or Advent is fairly simple, but you might cook certain foods at certain times of year or always bring hyacinths into school in January. I do this at home with my children –on a good year I plant hyacinth bulbs in November, keep them in the dark during December and bring them out when we take down the Christmas decorations on January 5th. On a bad year I nip down to the flower shop on January 4th. Either way, my children, whether they want to or not, will always associate the smell of hyacinth bulbs with new year's resolutions and new beginnings!

Flowers and food are the obvious ways to create these sense memories. Scented candles and oils would be another one to explore. If you don't want to burn oils for safety reasons make your own scent sprays by mixing essential oils with water and putting them in a spray gun. You might decide to always spray the carpet with jasmine oil before telling a story from the *Arabian Nights* – you will think of other links that appeal to you.

Another aspect of the physical environment to consider linking with the festivals is the auditory environment. What does the school sound like at this time of year? When children enter the school in the morning what do they hear? Up beat music? Positive music? Beautiful, soothing, calming music? It depends on the mood you want to create, because music is one of the most effective ways we have of influencing mood. Make links between certain music and the festivals, and the children will remember the festivals forever.

Strengths Builder: Treasure Chest

Start a treasure chest to prime your own environment. Fill it with mementoes and positive uplifting quotes and look at it at the start of lessons or at stressful moments.

Training Idea: Priming the school environment

Imagine you are all strangers to the school. Look around your school and ask yourselves what messages the environment sends. What messages do you want it to send?

PART THREE

The Festivals

NINE

Beginnings

A BEGINNINGS FESTIVAL is a way of setting the tone for the year to come, for clearly stating why you are all here and what you hope to achieve. It's a basic point, but do your pupils know why they come to school? Do they know why education is important? Does anyone ever tell them, in words of one syllable? Why do **you** think education is important? The Beginnings Festival would be a good time to think and talk about this as a community. It is a time for laying down positive habits of thought, speech and behaviour that will, by the end of the year, have become ingrained and automatic.

An amazingly successful American teacher, Marva Collins, whose inner city black pupils go on to become lawyers, doctors and, above all, teachers, uses simple aphorisms which the children learn to chant back to her to extraordinary effect. 'A rest from school is not a rest from what? She asks' 'FROM LEARNING!' they yell back. 'And what are you going to do over the summer?' she persists. 'READ 10 BOOKS,' they yell. A simple learning technique but it works. Think up some aphorisms of your own and use the Beginnings festival to begin to use them with the children.

I encourage schools to associate a colour and a kind of music with each festival and in early September, at the start of the school year, filling your school with the colour of sunshine and sunflowers, with cheerful music or bird song would seem appropriate.

The start of any new venture is full of hope and possibility – and of anxiety. The start of the academic year is no exception. We feel full of excitement – and full of trepidation and so do the children. Change is uncomfortable and the unknown can feel very scary.

Structure can help to alleviate anxiety so that change can be enjoyable. A mixture of the familiar and the new takes away some of the worry and allows children and adults to relax. Having Beginnings 'rituals' that are the same each year provides a little structure at what can be an anxious time. A 'First Day' assembly where the same song is sung each year, the same prayer said and the same story told would provide just this kind of familiar anchor.

Change is challenging and children's lives are changing all the time, because as children they are changing all the time. What makes change bearable is a feeling of being in control over some aspects of our life. This is difficult for children to feel because they are really not in control over very much of what they do, or of their environment. They are at school because they have to be, they spend much of the day doing what adults tell them to do in an environment designed by adults. They study a curriculum laid down by other adults who feel they know best what children should do with their time. Not a lot of choices there!

You can introduce little choices, however, especially at this time of year and increase children's sense of being in control and being able to affect the world around them, something that psychologists call 'self efficacy.' One important feature of pretend play, for example, is that it allows children to be 'in charge,' to create a character and a scenario and to do what they like with it. This sense of control may then translate into other contexts.

For younger children, plenty of pretend play is important at this time of year to increase their feelings of mastery over their environment and to give them choices. Other open ended activities provide a similar sense of 'being in charge.' The old fashioned 'Write a story, anything you like' instruction that teachers used to give before the national curriculum became more prescriptive allows children to take charge of their imagination and their work in a way that 'Write a mystery in the style of Joe Bloggs' does not. If you wish to help children feel in control and secure, more open ended instructions and opportunities to make choices in their work can achieve this.

The early days of each new class are essential for building relationships and for setting clear guidelines and a positive tone for the days that follow. You can begin to build 'traditions' for yourself and your class. Traditions like 'Mrs Eades is always at the door to greet us by name and shake hands with us at the start of the day' – the old fashioned custom of 'meet and greet' - would be a good one to start on the first day, for example. You might invent small customs for your class – we listen to music at the start of the day, on Mondays we share the very best bit from the weekend, during the first week of term we decide on our priorities for behaviour and draw up a new set of class rules, we take a few minutes to be quiet and listen to our breath so that we are calm and ready to learn.

I also think that food should be a part of a festival. A special food that you always bring into school for break time on the first day of term would be a positive start for many children.

Goal Setting is also an obvious tradition to keep at the start of the school year. You can set individual goals, class goals and school goals. Achieving goals can build optimism and facilitate the development of the strengths of this festival, love of learning, creativity and tolerance, so it is a Strengths Builder for all of these strengths. As a school you can decide on your collective goals for this year – a cross cultural link, an environmental project, a recycling commitment, a charitable project. Whole school goals can help build a sense of community as well as a vital belief in each person's ability to make a difference in the world. If setting goals for the whole school becomes a custom you follow at this time of year, and if everyone is invited to contribute to the process, all the children and all the adults in the community, then people will soon start offering suggestions. During the first week you can sift the suggestions and choose three goals for the year and announce them in assembly.

Teachers can share their own goals with their classes too. Why not let your students know that you have a personal goal to take more exercise this year, or to learn a new language or read a non fiction book once a week? As a class you might decide to undertake a charitable project, or to provide a particular service to the school community, or just to keep your classroom tidy so the cleaner looks forward to your particular room. You might decide to work on a particular strength together as a class and to keep track of how often you all manage to use that strength and whether, by the end of the year, you feel you have increased it.

You can lay down structures at this time of year that will provide security throughout the year. It can be satisfying to have echoes in beginnings and endings. The end of a term or a year can mirror the beginning – play a game on the first and last days of a term, for example or read a poem on the first day of the year and have as a goal learning it by heart to recite on the last day.

A lovely end of term assembly is 'Pearls', where each class shares with the rest of the school the highlight of the year. This can be echoed at the start of term by a 'Hopes' or 'Goals' assembly, when each class shares its goals for the year. One Headteacher I work with presents each class with a photo album on the first day of term. It is meant as place to record all the happiest and most exciting events of the year. At the end of that year, she shares one or two of the photos from each class with the whole school, a lovely echo from the beginning of the year that is satisfying and secure for the children.

Another way of using *Pearls* at the start of the year is as a Strengths Builder for creativity, love of learning or tolerance. It teaches children to savour and imprint happy memories in a very concrete way. Take time with them to remember the best part of the summer holiday – they can draw or write about it if you wish, as long as they also spend time simply remembering it, in as much colourful detail as they can. Then give each child a glass bead, what I call a 'magic memory pearl' and ask them to remember the best bit of the holiday in silence while they hold it, then to blow on the bead three times. That imprints the memory in the 'pearl'. When they are feeling sad or low or like giving up, holding the pearl will bring back that particular memory and lift their spirits.

Happy memories are an important resource for managing mood and emotion and for building resilience. Happy memories affect our mood in the present so bringing some into the beginnings festival is a good plan.

The strengths I have linked with the beginnings festival are what Peterson and Seligman call 'cognitive strengths' – strengths associated with thinking, knowledge and learning. These seem appropriate at the beginning of the academic year.

Creativity

Creativity is thinking of new ideas and novel ways of making or doing things. We can be creative in art and writing but equally in maths and science. Creativity and imagination are at the heart of all learning, not just in the arts but across the curriculum. We make creative choices when we get dressed in the morning or rearrange the furniture in the living room. Creativity does not mean that you must be good at art, but that you are willing to try new things in new ways, to think differently. Creativity involves thinking of original ideas or behaviours that are also useful, productive, beautiful, or life enhancing. Creativity feels good – creative people tend not to be motivated by money but by the joy of creation. When we create something, we take pride and pleasure in our creation whether or not it is an actual work of art. Creativity is closely linked to intrinsic motivation, a vital aspect of academic success.

It is not clear how to actively teach creativity, though the instruction 'be creative' has been shown to be effective. However, certain conditions encourage its development. One of these conditions is positive emotion – happier people are more capable of lateral and creative thinking, so using *Pearls* regularly through this festival might be a good idea. The *Mood Booster* Strengths Builder would also be appropriate, noticing the emotional aftertaste of events and activities and collecting and making a note of those that energise you, will be a good one to explore during this festival. If children want to do a creative piece of work they might take a minute or so to improve their mood first.

Other conditions that promote creativity are flexible teaching and free exploration without the worry of time constraints, an environment rich in books, music and art work, a playful attitude to learning, informality and openness.

Unfortunately it seems easier to inhibit creativity than to promote it. Time pressure, frequent critical examination, close supervision of work and the placing of limits on the possible range of solutions all undermine creativity – it is regrettable that these can be common conditions in today's classrooms.

Creative individuals tend to be risk takers and non conformists. Though the idea of the suffering creative genius is an enduring one, there is no necessary link between creativity and suffering. What there is, however, is a link between creativity and hard work. To produce a great work of artistic or scientific originality requires immense skill and hence years and years of effort.

Story Telling is a profoundly creative activity because each and every time you tell a story you create something new. It is therefore a Strengths Builder to use if you wish to promote creativity. A story telling teacher models creativity and story telling children learn that they can excel at being creative even if they can neither draw nor spell.

Philosophy is also a good activity to do regularly if you wish to focus on creativity because the students can learn to try out new ideas and opinions and to take risks, an essential element of being creative.

Opinion Lines are also a good way of fostering risk taking and individuality. You can do this with any statement about which children might have differing views. 'Best friends should never argue' or 'Too much telly is bad for you.' Make the statement and ask the children to stand in a line across the classroom depending on how much or how little they agree with the statement. Emphasise that you want to know what they think, not what their friend thinks, and that you are looking especially for independent thinkers, people who think for themselves. Shake a bell, or tap a drum, and ask the students to stand where they wish. Then talk with them a little about their opinions, reinforcing the value and importance of different points of view. The same activity is useful for focussing on another strength of this festival, tolerance, an ability to understand and consider different points of view.

Meditation has long been seen as a good way to encourage creativity. As such, simple calming exercises like *Listening to Your Breath*, or *Rain Stick Listening*, or *Rain Stick Walking* would be good to do regularly. For *Listening to Your Breath*, the children need to be sitting comfortably but with their backs straight. It helps when you first start to have quiet music playing. Then, speaking in a slow, calm voice say, "become aware of your body and where it touches the floor and the chair. Notice the feel of the surfaces beneath you. Place one hand gently inside the other and take a deep breath and let it out, letting your tension out as you do so. Now imagine a string pulling your head upwards so that your back is straight but relaxed. Now, think about your toes. Then give them a little wriggle and let them relax so they feel soft and warm, heavy and comfortable..... think of your whole feet....move them a little and then relax them, letting them feel soft and warm, heavy and comfortable.....think of your legs and let them relax...........and your tummy, notice it move as you breath softly in an out.................your back is straight but relaxed......your face is soft and you are smiling a little........your hands are heavy and relaxed, lying on your knees.........listen to your quiet breathing......in and out....in and out.........and as you listen to your breath it gets a little slower...a little longer.......you can listen to your breath...and lengthen your breath.........listen   to   your   breath...and   lengthen   your breath.....listen...and lengthen.....listen.....and lengthen.....

And open your eyes and give your body a wriggle to wake it up."

A different way of leading children into *Listening to Your Breath* is to omit the body scan and ask them to focus on the sound of the out breath, counting the breaths until they reach 10 and then starting again. This is a simple form of meditation described in an excellent book called *The Quiet* by Paul Wilson. If you wish to enjoy the many benefits of meditation for yourself this book is a good place to start.

Rain Stick Listening is also a simple introduction to meditation especially for younger children. The children can listen to the soothing sound of the beads. They can watch as they fall through the wheels. If you leave a second or two of silence before you turn the stick again, they begin to grow accustomed, little by little, to stillness and silence, something some people find very scary.

A rain stick walk can be an effective moving meditation. Say to the children that they are to walk slowly round the room imagining each foot sinking into soft sand while the beads fall. When the beads stop, they must stop too.

Or use the rain stick for '*Excellent Listening.*' Say, 'I'm looking for excellent listening' and when you see some, give the child the rain stick for a single turn. This works really well at quietening and calming a rowdy class, especially if you keep your voice low and your own movements slow and graceful.

If children want extra ideas for building or exploring their creativity on their own, these might include *Story Telling* and *Meditation*, certainly. Also they might play games like *Other Uses*, where you think of an object and then find new ways to use it. So, a book can become a coffee table if it's big enough or an umbrella or a hat or a door stop or a house for a mouse and so on. Or they could draw a dream, or play with colours on paper, build something new from construction materials then use the same materials and transform them into something else. Any activity that allows them to play, to explore, to take appropriate risks can use and build the frame of mind that allows us to create and so become a Strengths Builder for creativity.

An obvious genre of stories that indirectly reinforce creativity are creation myths. In ancient times creativity was closely associated with God or gods and Creator is another common term for God. There are many creation myths and these would be good to explore at the start of a school year. Besides the well known Judeo-Christian-Islamic myths, there are others, less well known and sometimes quite bizarre. One I like is an ancient Egyptian myth about the world starting when a god sneezes!

Another story you might tell to younger children to show creativity in action would be *The Gingerbread Man*, a lovely story of a creation that comes to life. *Rumpelstiltskin* is well known to younger children and, again, is a story about creativity, in this case turning straw into gold. What is less well known is that there are many different versions of this story. In fact, wherever you find spinning, you find a Rumpelstiltskin story though the character and the task varies. Older students might research other versions, the English *Tom Tit Tot*, for example, or the Scottish *Mollie Whuppie*. On Orkney, the Rumpelstiltskin story has been combined with another Scandinavian tale to produce the rather gory, but very funny, *Peerie Fool*. Analysing the different features of these tales could lead to pupils producing their own '*Rumpelstiltskin*' set in the modern day.

Love of Learning

The Chinese have a single word for love of learning – *hao-xue-xin* – which translates in English as the 'heart and mind for wanting to learn.' Notice that both heart and mind are involved. Learning is cognitive, but it is also profoundly emotional. Unless we feel some level of emotional engagement with the material we need to learn – and for the people we learn with and from - we will struggle to master anything. We have to 'want' to learn and 'wanting,' of course, is about emotions.

A love of learning is at the heart of education and, predictably, children who love learning do well at school. Though for some people, love of learning is a general strength, most people enjoy learning something and a specific interest such as cooking or PE may be used to foster a more general love of learning.

I have combined two of Peterson and Seligman's strengths here, love of learning and curiosity. They both relate to the desire to discover and experience new things and an enjoyment of learning. Both are associated with positive results, like pleasure, good mental health, the ability to persist in the face of frustration, even aging well.

Curiosity has negative as well as positive associations. There is the curiosity that kills the cat, a prying nosiness or the extreme risk taker or thrill seeker that endangers themselves and others. It is the positive curiosity we focus on here, the curiosity that wants to learn more about the world and people and which brings an added zest to the dullest day. Satisfying our curiosity, learning or finding out something new, produces feelings of competence and well-being, which leads to further curiosity, a virtuous circle. Curiosity is one of the strengths most strongly linked to happiness and a satisfying life. The curious person is less likely to report feelings of stress or boredom and more likely to be creative, to enjoy challenges in work and play, and to enjoy education.

There is always anxiety attached to learning new things and so the curious person is someone who can tolerate anxiety and who feels secure enough to cope with uncertainty. A lack of security as a young child may inhibit curiosity. Children and teenagers who declare something to be 'boring' may actually lack the courage to explore something unknown and challenging. The anxiety seems too much to bear.

Creating a safe and structured classroom environment is one way teachers can facilitate the development of curiosity – feeling nervous of a teacher's reaction – or of fellow pupils' reactions – will certainly inhibit free expression or questioning. It is vital that everyone in the group is respectful of opinions, questions and statements, however wild and off the wall!

In my sessions I operate a zero tolerance on laughing at remarks – unless the remark was clearly meant to be funny. Mocking laughter is a subtle but very aggressive way of attacking one another and will discourage open intellectual exploration and risk taking like nothing else.

Philosophy is a very important activity for encouraging curiosity and a love of learning. It is an excellent way of creating a safe learning environment and for laying down the rules of polite but vigorous academic debate. A class that regularly uses philosophy will produce children who respect one another's views and know how to challenge and to be challenged in a civilised manner. It is also an excellent way of exploring curiosity. Children are curious about everything and philosophy sessions let *them* ask questions for a change and explore what they wish – you keep them on track and facilitate discussion but otherwise you let them go, in their debate and in their imaginations, wherever they want to go.

Interestingly, it is not just feelings like fear and guilt or worry about 'getting it wrong' that diminish curiosity, but also external rewards. Stickers and prizes do not, it seems, really encourage genuine curiosity about the world, but focus attention away from the wonder of learning to the desire to please others, to beat others, or just to earn the reward.

Love of learning is closely associated, like curiosity and creativity, with intrinsic motivation. Again, the most successful learners are those who focus on the mastery of skills rather than on outcomes, on improved effort and ability rather than grades or 'coming first'. This means, for teachers, that it is vital that most praise is given for effort and improvement rather than achievement. The child who is told, 'That is an excellent essay' may start to feel that it has to achieve an essay equally good to earn your good opinion and so actually feel discouraged. Some children may feel that if they drop below 'excellent' at any point then they cease to be worthwhile – it is the route many perfectionists and high achievers have travelled. Conversely, the child who is told, 'You worked really hard at that' knows that he or she can always work equally hard, though the next essay may not be quite up to the standard of the first. We cannot always come first or guarantee an A*, but we can all try hard and gradually improve. Praise of effort, rather than achievement, builds more resilient and self confident learners.

Love of learning does not develop in a vacuum. Psychologists argue that talent rarely flourishes without encouragement and recognition. Teachers are vital in creating and sustaining a love of learning in children. They can do this most successfully by creating safe learning environments in which children and students are encouraged to ask questions, in which they can help to plan and take charge of their own learning, and where failure is a normal, even welcome part of the learning process.

Crucially, teachers also need to be cultivating and passing on their own love of learning. The children we teach will probably not remember the content of our lessons when they are in middle age. They will remember our passion, though, our interest in them, our delight in their progress and successes, our love of our subjects. We teach by our enthusiasm, our enthusiasm for the children themselves and for learning. It is vital that we make as much time as possible to do the things we really love in our classrooms, so that children experience our genuine interest at first hand. That is how, more than anything, we will instil in children a life long love of learning – by nurturing it within ourselves, first.

A classroom activity like *What's New?* can be an enjoyable and practical way to encourage love of learning. In the morning you all set a goal to learn at least one new thing by home time – spell or read a word, learn a word in another language, find out a new fact, learn a new game. At home time you report back on what you have learned and cheer one another accordingly. If the whole school takes part it becomes a way of highlighting the central role and pleasure of learning in your community – a Learn Something New Day, a tradition for this festival.

Individual ideas for Strengths Builders would be activities like 'learn a new word to spell or read' or 'look up a long word in a dictionary and learn its definition' or 'ask an adult to remember a game they played as a child and to teach it to you'. Other ideas would be to encourage the exploration of new foods or to return to old fashioned learning by heart, learn a poem or a song or a story to tell.

Stories that indirectly reinforce the strengths of love of learning and curiosity are those that have a character going out into the world to explore. *The Three Pigs* is a suitable one for the youngest children. *The Three Feathers* has a similar structure and theme but is less well known and suited to older children or teenagers. Using *What Went Well* as a kind of story, telling the children the story of *What Went Well Today* as a way of closing a session or day, will also encourage positive attitudes to learning. If you do this often enough, the children will learn to do it themselves, too and combine oral story telling with helping you to build a positive learning community.

Tolerance

The strength of tolerance is based on Peterson and Seligman's strength of open-mindedness, the ability to consider view points other than one's own and to carefully weigh ideas that are different to or contradict our own ideas. Open mindedness corrects a near universal tendency which psychologists call 'my side bias', the tendency only to notice evidence that supports what we already think.

Open mindedness can increase with age and education but does not always, so it is worth considering how we might create an environment in which it flourishes. *Philosophy with Children* is one way that we can actively promote the practice of looking at evidence for and against our own views. It encourages reflection, actively looking for at least one counter argument to a view and then considering it. Argument, of the kind encouraged by philosophy, must be seen as worthwhile before people will engage in it. Teachers can show best by example that they value the willingness to consider alternatives and even to change one's mind in the face of good arguments.

Open mindedness has been shown to lead to better academic scores and to help individuals resist suggestion and manipulation and to cope with stress.

One way of building this strength is through a Strengths Builder such as *Same /Different,'* which can help children develop the habit of noticing and accepting differences. At its simplest level, children work with a friend to find as many ways in which they are the same as possible, and as many ways in which they are different as possible. A more complex version would be to take an issue like 'Eating meat is wrong,' and to find as many arguments for and against as they can.

Story telling involves the narrator in considering and identifying with each character in turn, so working on stories can help in promoting an awareness of different points of view. *Good Bits / Bad Bits* is a game that can follow any story. Again you can play it at different levels depending on the age of the children. Young children can simply think of 'A bit they liked' and 'A bit they didn't like'. If you collect their ideas, you will inevitably find that some children liked one bit and others disliked the same bit. Pointing this out to children, not as a source of concern, but as a point of interest and value, helps them to begin to understand that people think differently – and that this thinking differently is something positive.

The next stage in this game is to consider the actions of the story from the point of view of a character within it. What did Jack enjoy? What didn't Jack enjoy? A further stage is to consider the story from the point of view of a third character. What did the giant enjoy? What didn't the giant enjoy? One story, many different views.

Another aspect to tolerance and open mindedness is being tolerant of ourselves and allowing ourselves to fail. There are some children who are very hard on themselves, who think they should never feel angry, or frightened, or sad, or that they should never fail in their work. Learning to be gentle with others is important. Learning to be gentle with ourselves is a mark of emotional maturity. *Meditation* and *Mood Booster* can be used to teach children explicitly to look after themselves in this way.

A third aspect of open mindedness is the cultivation of clear thinking. We all think in a muddled and overly pessimistic way at times. Something goes wrong and we think 'The universe hates me.' We have a row with a friend and we think, 'I'm hopeless at friendship.' Sometimes called 'catastrophising' or simply a 'pessimistic explanatory style,' you can play games with children that will encourage you and them to think in a more balanced and positive way. *Eeyore Thoughts* is one such game.

An idea I have borrowed from my colleague, the business consultant Amanda Levy, is *WOW*, which stands for Wishing Others Well. Amanda uses it in customer service training. I have adapted it for the maelstrom of school life. It can be really difficult to feel positive towards people when they disagree with us. Practising positive thoughts as a game can make it easier to do it in the heat of real life. Ask children to relax, play some soft music and then ask them to imagine a friend and to picture themselves giving something good to this friend as a gift. Now ask them to imagine someone who is *not* their friend and to imagine that they are a super kind hero, brave and noble and can give this non-friend something just as good as they gave their friend.

Turn the *WOW* idea into a concrete form by printing WOW cards and letting children use them to send compliments, thank you's and kind words to people in school. You could start a custom of sending a WOW card on the first and last days of a term and sending them to

NOT friends – other people who can also be treated with kindness and respect.

Suggestions for building tolerance and open-mindedness for individuals to work on alone might include ideas such as 'Play with someone you have argued with' or 'Find someone who disagrees with you about something and play with them'. Simply, 'Play with/talk to someone you don't know well' or 'Find someone different from you and have a conversation' can also be useful. Older students can benefit from 'Read a newspaper you won't agree with.' Games that encourage pupils to collect different views, or to find as many different favourite films as possible, will also encourage the concept that diversity is valuable.

There is an old traditional story I knew as a child as *The Blind Men and the Elephant*. I retell it as 'What is an elephant really like?' and have six people in the dark trying to work out what an elephant is like from just touching part of it. I avoid having the people as blind because I am not keen on the metaphor of physical blindness for intolerance and ignorance. Anyway, here is my version:

What is an elephant really like?

In the days before television was invented, in the days before cameras had even been thought of, there lived in an Indian village six people who had never seen an elephant.

They had heard of elephants. They had heard that elephants were huge and powerful and could move tree trunks and lift rocks. They had heard that elephants were wise and gentle and that children could ride upon their backs. They had heard that elephants were fierce and dangerous and could kill a man with one blow. But they had never seen an elephant for themselves.

One day a traveller came to the village and told them that he had seen an elephant by a watering hole near by. The six people were very excited. At last they would find out for themselves what an elephant was really like. They were so excited they set out at once though it was late in the evening. By the time they reached the watering hole the sun had set and darkness covered the land. It was pitch black and the six people could not see anything at all, not a thing. They moved slowly, with their hands out in front of them to stop them from falling.

And one by one they found the elephant.

The first person whose name was *(you could put in a child's name here)*.......touched one part of the elephant and said, 'An elephant is really like a snake, a long, fat snake'. *(For younger children you could point to a trunk on a picture or model of an elephant, or whisper 'he had found the ....' and let the children supply the word)*

The second person, whose name was.........touched another part of the elephant and said, 'An elephant is really like a spear, a sharp pointed spear.' (Tusk)

The third person, whose name was........touched another part of the elephant and said, 'An elephant is like a tree trunk, a fat stumpy tree trunk.' (Leg)

The fourth person, whose name was.........touched another part of the elephant and said, 'An elephant is really like a wall, a huge broad wall.' (Body)

The fifth person whose name was .....touched another part of the elephant and said, 'An elephant is really like a rope, a thin wispy rope.' (Tail)

The sixth and last person, whose name was......touched another part of the elephant and said, 'An elephant is really like a sheet, a thin sheet flapping in the wind.' (Ear)

The six people argued that each of them was right and the others were wrong. They argued and they argued and they argued, all night long. When the sun came up they finally saw what the elephant was really like ....which of them was right?

TEN

Thanksgiving, Harvest, Sukkot or Raksha Bandhan

ARVEST FESTIVALs are not a particularly old Christian custom in Britain – they were invented by a Victorian clergyman. However the custom of giving thanks for food and for the harvest in particular is an ancient one common to many faiths and traditions. Americans rightly value Thanksgiving as a high point of the year. Harvest festivals have taken place in churches and schools in Britain for over a hundred years. The Jewish festival of Sukkot, also known as the Feast of Tabernacles, is a time of rejoicing for the harvest. For Hindus, there is a strong element of thanks giving and gratitude in the celebration of Raksha Bandhan, when brothers and sisters exchange friendship bracelets to show appreciation for one another. Which tradition you choose to emphasise is up to you, but all of them provide an appropriate opportunity to focus on and build the strengths of gratitude, generosity and fairness.

Coming together as a school community to focus on the good things you share and to say thank you for them, is a powerful act. Different faiths may adapt the thanksgiving accordingly – we thank God or Allah or we cultivate 'thankfulness'. The act of rejoicing, of giving thanks, binds us together and builds us up.

This would also be an appropriate festival for looking outwards at the needs of the world and at beginning or continuing a major fundraising project. The strength of gratitude leads naturally to generosity, so some kind of charitable focus would be entirely appropriate for this festival.

Another focus you might choose would be hospitality. Hospitality, sharing our time and food with others, is an important tradition in all faiths and it is a skill that children and young people need to learn. Putting others first, planning an event with others in mind, not primarily ourselves, is an important social ability. Individual classes or the school as a whole can prioritise hospitality at this time of year.

Linked to hospitality is cooking and, specifically, baking. I am a firm believer in every person in this country knowing how to bake bread *without* a bread maker! It is very simple, very satisfying, a basic human ability and experience, and a very calming one. You might almost include bread making as another meditation, though I haven't here. What I have done at the end of the chapter is to provide you with a simple recipe that will make four small bread rolls, enough to eat and share with someone else. This might form the basis of inviting another class or a group from outside school to lunch.

Hospitality can be as simple or as elaborate as you wish. One school I work with runs a weekly luncheon club for elderly people in the area. The eleven year olds in the school serve the guests and sit and chat with them and both groups benefit enormously. If you did not feel able to do this weekly, the Thanksgiving festival would be an excellent opportunity to do something of this kind once a year.

Gratitude

Gratitude is one of the key strengths for enjoying life. A grateful person is not just someone who remembers to say 'thank you', though they do. Crucially, a grateful person focuses on the good things they have rather than on the things they do not have – they are the antithesis of the envious person who struggles to 'keep up with the Jones' or the entitled person who thinks life owes them a living. Grateful people focus less on material wealth and are more likely to share their possessions with others. They are more open, more willing to accept commitment to and responsibility for others and less prone to mental health problems than their less grateful counter parts. There even appears to be growing evidence that they are healthier and live longer!

Gratitude is one of Peterson and Seligman's 'transcendent' strengths, strengths that connect us with something beyond ourselves and which add meaning and value to life. It includes the capacity to notice and wonder at the ordinary – at clean water in our taps, at the colours of spring, at a kind word – and to take nothing for granted. Gratitude enhances personal well-being and builds good relationships – expressing appreciation for a spouse and for what they do has been shown to be a corner stone of a happy marriage. Gratitude involves someone other than ourselves – we are grateful to a person or to God or to life itself. A person who resists any sense of needing others will struggle to feel grateful.

Gratitude is strongly associated with happiness and good health and even with academic success. In a study, adults kept a gratitude journal, recording each night three things they felt grateful for. Control groups recorded neutral events or complaints about the day. The gratitude journal produced higher reported levels of energy, enthusiasm, determination, attentiveness and alertness – such a practice may therefore build optimism and happiness.

You can build on this finding by keeping a *Class Gratitude Journal* and, at the end of the day, record what the children and what you have enjoyed about the day. At the end of the week you could use this to recap on what has been positive for everyone. *WWW, What Went Well?* is another way of doing this exercise and, done regularly, may help children to focus on what has been good, balancing our normal human tendency to notice what goes wrong, what psychologists call our 'negativity bias'.

It seems that seeing oneself as a passive victim precludes a sense of gratitude. *Change the World* is a Strengths Builder that may address this tendency by encouraging the class to think of a way of making the world a little better. You might do this by fund raising, picking up litter, recycling – whatever the children suggest. It can be long term – supporting a village in the developing world – or short term – tidying the school TODAY. One goal of this activity is the understanding that little changes add up to big changes and one person does make a difference – we are not helpless, we can do things to change the world.

Reflection and the ability to savour experiences may also encourage gratitude. *Pearls* would be a good Strengths Builder to continue with, boosting the ability to anchor and return to happy memories. A particular kind of meditation called *Savouring* is usually a favourite with children – it can involve food. We live our lives at a rapid pace and rarely stop to pay full attention to what we are doing. Savouring slows us down and lets us enjoy a moment to the full.

We can savour foods – either sweet or savoury - by eating something slowly together as a class. Hand round the food, ask the children just to hold it and look at it and think about it. Then, when everyone is ready, eat together in silence, concentrating just on the taste and texture of what you are eating. A silent 'thank you' for the food is a good end to this activity.

You can also savour other things. On a crisp autumn morning go out together and stand in silence for a minute or so and savour the blue of the sky, or the sounds of birds.

Just stopping and directing the children's full attention to something can lift mood and enhance pleasure. It is also, interestingly, a community building activity because for that moment everyone has a common focus. Enjoy each experience as much as you can. Return to it at the end of the day as a *Pearl* and implant it in your magic memory pearl.

Silent Thank You can have quite an effect on a school. I first taught children the British sign language gesture for 'thank you' as an appropriate response to oral story telling. You put your hand to your face, fingers against the chin and then move it downwards. When I have told a story I thank the children, silently, for listening and they thank me for the story. It is a quiet, reflective end to a story or session and infinitely better than applause or a loud chorus of 'thank you Jenny!' The schools I demonstrated this in have developed it further. Children are encouraged to use a silent thank you to one another when they have worked in pairs or groups, to their teachers at the end of a day, to dinner ladies and kitchen staff. The incidence of 'thank you's' around the schools have increased noticeably.

If you wish to gear some *Story Telling* towards gratitude you could ask children to pick a story they have really enjoyed hearing and to retell that. Working in pairs they might offer help to one another since we have to be prepared to give in order to receive. In a *Philosophy* session you might focus on appreciating, being grateful for, our ability to think and reason and for the views of other people, whether similar to our own or not. You might also discuss the nature and importance of gratitude.

Revive the art of *Thank You Letters* as a class. Write them regularly through the festival, to one another, to dinner ladies, former teachers, parents. Encourage the children to see thank you letters as an important part of relationship building.

Children can do some of the Strengths Builders on their own as well as as a class. Other things they might do individually would be to draw *Thank You Pictures*, pictures of what is good in life, or to eat lunch and *savour* it. Researching the religious practice of '*Grace*' before meals would be fun, there would be thanksgiving prayers from different faiths that they could learn and use. A good resource to use would be *Seasons of Thanks: Graces and Blessings for Every Home*, by Taz Tagore.

Stories that might be told to reinforce the strength of gratitude include the biblical story of *The Ten Lepers* and a lovely North American Indian story, *The Spirit of the Corn*, which I include at the end of this chapter.

Generosity

Generosity flows naturally from gratitude. Grateful people have been found to be more generous and that is understandable since a focus on the good things you have will tend to encourage you to feel you have plenty to share.

Generosity is closely related to the strength of kindness, one of the interpersonal strengths. However, these interpersonal strengths are so important it seems appropriate to focus on them more than once and generosity fits particularly well with the themes of thanksgiving and giving to others.

Generosity benefits the giver as much as the recipient. Evidence suggests that kind and generous people enjoy better physical and mental health and live longer than their more selfish counterparts. Kindness, generosity and care for others are at the heart of all major world religions and philosophical traditions and are universally valued as important. Despite this, little work has been done on how these to encourage these strengths in children.

One interesting piece of research indicates that kindness is related to mood and people who feel cheerful are far more inclined to kind acts than unhappy ones. This may also be true of generosity. For this reason the Strengths Builders that aim to improve mood, such as *Savouring, Rain Stick Meditation, Listen to Your Breath, Mood Booster, Treasure Chest, WWW* and *Pearls* can all be used to boost our 'generosity impulse.' *Change the World* is an obvious Strengths Builder to use around the time of harvest.

Since we get more of what we focus on, an explicit focus on generosity will tend to increase it. Noticing and commenting on generosity in the classroom will make it more visible. *Reflections* would be a useful Strengths Builder to use. You can use *Reflections* with any strength. Simply spend a moment or two at the end of the day or the week thinking about how, if at all, you have used the strength of generosity. Children can share their reflections with others if they wish but not if they do not wish to. It will focus attention on their own use of a particular strength. You might combine this with thinking of new ways to use the strength tomorrow so that those who haven't used it today realise that they can choose to be generous. It will be important to include a broad range of ideas – they can be generous by sharing things, their time, their attention, their sympathy. Once they see that generosity can involve something as small and as possible as a smile or a helping hand with something heavy, they will feel more inclined to practice it. The deliberate decision to be kind, to be generous is always a valuable one to make.

Baking and *Invitations* are important Strengths Builders for giving children practical skills in being generous. Making someone a loaf of bread is a simple but generous gift – it takes time and love to make good bread. The recipe at the end of this chapter will make four small rolls, one to eat and one to give away. Encourage the children to knead the dough with love, to think of the person they will give it to as they do so. Jamie Oliver shocked the health and safety lobby when he told the school cook in his *Jamie's School Dinners* television series on school dinners that she should always kiss the dough before she baked it! Quite right too!

Generosity focuses attention away from the self and on to the other person. *Invitations* is a Strengths Builder that aims to give children an opportunity to do this and to practice the skill of hospitality – because it is a skill and it can be learned. First, you have to think of a person or group of people to invite to visit you. It might be another class of older or younger pupils, or a teacher or some of your support staff – how often does the caretaker get invited to parties in school? Then you think of something you can do for them that they might enjoy – a new song, a poem, a short play, or just a chat about a topic they are interested in. You think of some simple food they might enjoy – you can easily combine this activity with *Baking* for example. You write invitations that will make them wish to come along, you decorate the room simply but pleasantly. Such activities would cover a variety of curriculum areas in an imaginative way (including RE, since hospitality is a key concept in all faiths) and also provide the opportunity for everyone to give generously of their time, talents and good will.

Additional generosity Strengths Builders that children could do individually might be sharing a toy, game or piece of equipment, helping out in the dinner hall, helping a parent or carer without being asked, using their time generously, making or buying a gift to cheer somebody up.

There are excellent stories that reflect the strength of generosity. The story of St Bridget is one – she got into terrible trouble for giving away her family's bread and her father's valuable sword.

Fairness

Fairness is one of Peterson and Seligman's strengths of justice, interpersonal strengths that determine how we relate to groups beyond our immediate circle, though fairness is also important for our closest relationships.

People with a well developed sense of fairness report more career fulfilment, continue to learn throughout their lives, are actively involved in their communities and are less prone to immoral and anti social behaviour.

There are two elements to fairness. One is justice – the logical application of rules of right and wrong, and the other is care, what is right and good for the other person. The development of a sense of justice is seen as passing through definite and predictable stages. Very young children think of what is right in an ego centric way – what is right is what benefits them or what avoids getting them into trouble. The next stage considers close relationships – what is right is what benefits friends and family. Then the wider society is considered and finally abstracts concepts of universal justice and fairness.

The care aspect of fairness, by contrast, is concerned more with relationships and the needs, interests and well-being of the other person, it involves compassion and emotional sensitivity.

It is thought that fairness, sometimes called 'moral judgement' develops best in people who love learning, who like challenges and stimulation, who are able to think deeply about themselves and others, who make plans and set goals for themselves and who think about

and they can benefit from safe and useful discussion of feelings and motives without making themselves vulnerable. *Good Bits / Bad Bits* would also be a good Strengths Builder to encourage this awareness of the thoughts and feelings of others.

The Little Red Hen is an obvious story about fairness for young children – older ones might consider the question of whether what she did was fair in the end? *Goldilocks* would also stimulate thought about questions of fairness. Older children would enjoy *Rumpelstiltskin* stories – again they touch on issues of fairness.

Individual Strengths Builders to include in your strength gym to exercise fairness might include 'Involve other people in a game, not just best friends,' or 'Run a game and make sure everyone follows the rules.'

The Spirit of the Corn

In a land far away and long ago, there was a village where the sun always shone, and the rain always fell, and the soil was rich and fertile, and the corn grew and grew and grew, and there was lots to eat.

There was so much to eat, in fact, that the people grew careless. They forgot to work in the fields, so the weeds grew.

They forgot to store their corn carefully, in baskets or holes in the ground, so the mice got in and stole it, and the rain came in and made the corn rot away.

Worst of all, they forgot to say thank you to the spirit of the corn.

In all the village, there was only one man who remembered to weed his fields. Who remembered to store his corn carefully in baskets and holes in the ground. Who remembered to say thank you to the spirit of the corn. And his name was Dayohagwenda.

One day, Dayohagwenda was walking in the forest when he met an old man, sitting by a hut full of holes and surrounded by weeds. The man was dressed in rags and he was weeping.

'Grandfather, why are you weeping?' asked Dayohagwenda.

'I am weeping,' the old man said, 'because your people have forgotten to weed my corn. Because they have forgotten to store my corn carefully in baskets or holes in the ground. Because they have forgotten to say thank you for the corn.'

Dayohagwenda realised that this was not an ordinary old man. This was the spirit of the corn and he was weeping because he thought he had been forgotten.

Dayohagwenda rushed back to his village where the people were on the edge of starvation and close to death. He told them what he had seen. He told them what he had heard. He told them that the spirit would help them if they remembered him, again.

Then Dayohagwenda dug up his own corn and found that there was more there, than when he stored it away. He shared it with his people so that they did not starve.

And after that, the sun always shone, and the rain always fell and the corn grew and grew, and the people of the village remembered to work in the fields and dig up the weeds. They remembered to store the corn carefully in baskets or holes in the ground. And, most important of all, they remembered to say thank you to the spirit of the corn.

Baking – Makes four bread rolls, two to eat and two to share

Bread has an important place in many cultural traditions and is both simple and rewarding to make. This recipe makes four large bread rolls, enough for a child and one guest, so each child can share food they have made themselves. It can be made in a morning ready for lunch.

200g flour (2/3 white and 1/3 wholemeal makes a nice mix)

Quarter pint of water

1 sachet easy blend yeast

1 teaspoon salt

1 dessert spoon vegetable oil

- Combine ingredients and mix to a dough – the amount of water will vary slightly depending on the flour.

- Knead for 5 minutes.

- Encourage the children to knead silently and enjoy the texture and feel of the dough.

- Shape dough into four rolls and place on an oiled baking tray.

- Cover with a damp tea towel and leave to rise in a warm place for about an hour.

- You can sprinkle extra flour on the rolls before you bake them, or poppy seeds or sesame seeds or oats, or glaze them with milk if you prefer.

- Bake at Gas Mark 7/ 425°F/ 220°C for 15 minutes and tip onto a cooling rack.

- When the bread has cooled, it can be served with fillings, as sandwiches, or to accompany a simple soup.

ELEVEN

Festivals of Light: Advent, Divali, Hannukah, Eid

ADVENT, WHICH LITERALLY translates as 'arrival' or 'coming,' is an ancient tradition of the Christian church, a time of waiting and reflection. Advent itself is not a feast, but traditionally a time of fasting before the feast of Christmas. It is a time of preparation, of looking inwards. The Christian is reflecting not just on the arrival of the Christ child at Christmas, but also on the arrival of Christ the king at the end of time. Christians look back at the ancient Christmas story and the birth of Christ 2000 years ago. They also look forward to the end of all things, and a new heaven and a new earth.

In today's era of instant gratification, fast food and rapid communications, a time of waiting and reflection might feel rather quaint and old fashioned. However, there is an ancient wisdom in balancing action with reflection, feasting with fasting, and taking time out of busyness to be still. In schools, the run up to Christmas can feel frenetic and very stressful. The Advent festival in Celebrating Strengths started with the aim of having a longer but more measured build up to Christmas and a gentler more reflective pace to the term.

It does achieve this. Schools that use the whole of the month before the holiday to keep Advent have reported a more peaceful and spiritual flavour to the term and a calmer end of term for the children. In addition to this, you are teaching the children some valuable life skills – one of which is waiting itself. The ability to delay gratification and to control impulses is an important aspect of a healthy emotional life - it contributes to academic achievement and will contribute to good health and financial stability in later life. Another important feature of an emotionally mature life is self awareness, learning to look inwards and understand what we are feeling and how to manage our emotions.

A festival that has reflection as a key aspect will encourage children to value this aspect of life – they will see that the adults around them enjoy the opportunity to be still and quiet and will come to accept that quiet times are an important part of life. The key elements of looking back – savouring happy memories – and looking forward – setting goals and being optimistic about the future - are both built into this festival through a variety of Strengths Builders.

The Advent festival has magical elements to it – the spiral and the central story of *The Road to Bethlehem*. One of its key aims is to build happy memories for children to look back on, since having a storehouse of happy memories is an important element in becoming a resilient adult. It also aims to increase enjoyment for both adults and children, building again on the fact that positive emotion helps us to learn and to work more effectively.

The Advent festival is rooted in the Christian tradition. However, there are other festivals held during the dark days of November and December that also make use of the symbolism of lights and which could be incorporated into a festival held at this time of year. Eid is one, Hannukah another, Divali a third. The spiral walk which is the key Strengths Builder would adapt to traditions other than the Christian one. Work with children or adults of those faith traditions to incorporate stories and traditions from their own festivals into a Festival of Light, in a way that feels authentic to believers from each faith, something that I have done with my colleague Reena Govindji, a Hindu, at CAPP.

The strengths we focus on during Advent or a festival of light are hope, spirituality and humour. Hope is an essential element of all faith traditions and a key element of education too. Without hope in the future there would be no point in acquiring an education – teachers are by nature hopeful people, because their very profession is forward looking. Children learn to hope because we are hopeful for them. Spirituality seems an appropriate strength to focus on during a festival of Advent or light. Spiritual awareness is a part of a healthy and balanced life but it is a part of life that can be difficult to make space for in a crowded school day. Time and space to think about the important and deeper aspects of life are built into this festival.

Humour is also included. Like hope and spirituality it is one of Peterson and Seligman's 'transcendent' strengths, strengths that connect us to something bigger than ourselves and which help to provide meaning in life. The Advent festival has solemn moments, moments to look inward and reflect while humour takes us out of ourselves and provides balance and perspective. Spirituality or religion without humour can be rather deadly.

Hope and Optimism

Hope and optimism are forward looking strengths, a belief that the future will contain more good than bad and that we can influence it ourselves to make good things more likely. They are not just *beliefs*, they are also *emotions*, positive feelings that feel good in themselves and which energise and motivate us. Also, beyond beliefs and emotions, hope and optimism lead to *actions* which will bring about desired goals.

Encouraging optimism and hope is worthwhile on many levels. Though we may have an inherited tendency to be more or less optimistic, we can learn ways to increase our level of optimism and to influence those around us. Optimism has many positive results – academic success being one of them. Others are better relationships, better health, less depression, more perseverance and effective problem solving and even longer life.

There are different ways of considering hope and optimism. One considers people's attitudes to goals, looking at two aspects of goal setting, the first being the determination to achieve the goal (I *will* do it) and the second being the pathway to achieve the goal (and this is the *way* I will do it). This can be referred to as will power and way power thinking and is incorporated into a Strengths Builder called *Where There's a Will…….*

Children are encouraged to set goals for themselves – this week goals, this term goals, this year goals, in the future goals. For each goal they set they need to think of the 'way' there, the path. They might even draw the goal as a destination at the end of a road, or a map with the 'way' marked on it and the 'will' or the goal, at the end of the path. The 'way' has foot steps on it, each step being a stage toward achievement of the final goal. You could get creative with this and award foot step shaped certificates whenever a 'step on the way' is achieved – or better still, children make their own 'step' certificates and award them to themselves when they achieve those steps. The steps need to follow the advice of the acronym SMART in being Specific, Measurable, Achievable, Realistic and Timely targets.

Learning how to set goals, how to break down those goals into achievable steps, how to work hard at reaching each step *and* to celebrate the achievement of each step in turn, is an important aspect of building a hopeful, happy and effective outlook on life. You do not sit around waiting for someone else to do it for you, you decide where you want to go and what you want to do, what you have to do to get there and then you work hard to bring it about!

Another way of thinking about optimism considers the way we explain bad events to ourselves, the stories we tell ourselves in the face of failure or setback or unhappy events. Optimistic thinking – a positive habit of thought - can be learned and passed on. Stories, especially traditional ones, are hopeful by their nature, so using stories in *Story Telling* and *Create a Story Space* can be Strengths Builders for hope. *Cinderella* is a particularly nice one for Christmas. *Eeyore Thoughts* is a Strengths Builder for optimism, as are *Pearls* and *WWW* and all kinds of meditation. What is vital is that you take *action* to change attitudes. You may wish to be more optimistic and happier, but unless you do something to bring this about, your good intentions will not last. You should strive to build positive habits of thought, speech and behaviour. As such, the Strengths Builders are important for teachers and other adults, first and foremost, and then second for the children with whom we work. Find one you like, build it into your routine, and then you are more likely to see lasting change.

The *Spiral* is a simple walking meditation that is lovely for encouraging optimistic thinking and space for reflection. The *Spiral* is based on an ancient Christian form of prayer – that of walking a labyrinth. One of the most famous labyrinths is in The Cathedral of Our Lady of Chartres, France. Monastic cloisters were built along similar principles to allow a slow, walking prayer to take place, whereby the physical journey made by the body along the path or labyrinth mirrors the spiritual journey of the soul.

In the schools we build the simplest kind of labyrinth, the spiral. The spiral is built before the children enter the hall and a lighted candle placed at its centre. The children enter a darkened hall, with a single candle lit and quiet music playing. The adult who will guide them through the spiral should already be seated on the outside of the spiral and the children should arrive quiet and ready to begin. They sit around the outside of the spiral behind an unlit tea light in a holder.

The guide welcomes the children and explains that they are going to walk the spiral. Older children and teenagers can be told that this is an ancient prayer form and a variety of walking meditation. Younger ones can be told that it is a 'special walk,' a spiral, but they may also want to learn that it is a walking meditation. Invite them to think of what they wish as they walk it – it is their spiral walk – but they may wish to take a happy memory into the spiral and as they walk out, to contemplate a hope or a goal.

The guide enters the spiral first carrying their own unlit tea light and sits down by the candle and then the children walk in one by one, carrying their tea lights. There will be two children in the spiral at any one time, one entering and one leaving. They soon learn when to stand and begin their own walk so the adult guide can monitor the pace very gently.

In the centre of the spiral the adult guide lights the tea light and returns it to the child, making eye contact and giving a light physical touch as they return the candle. When the adult in the centre lights the candle for each child they can, if they are comfortable, use the ancient prayer that Christians have used for centuries at this time of year *'The light of Christ in glory shining scatter the darkness from before your path.'* For younger children you might just say, *'Amy, a Christmas light shining just for you.'*

When the children reach the outside of the spiral they carry their candle back to their place and sit down, placing it in front of them. As more children and adults walk the spiral, the outer circle of light grows until it is completed by the adult in the spiral walking out and taking their own place in the outer circle. Then adults and children together sit and enjoy the lights!

What fascinates me about the spiral is both how simple and how profound an experience it is. It is a great privilege to hand children a candle and see their faces light up (no pun intended!). It is also a privilege to provide a group of adults and children together with a little bit of time for quiet reflection. Sometimes when we have done this the memories the children have brought to the spiral have not been happy ones – or not purely happy ones. It is not uncommon for them to turn to me at the end and say, 'I was thinking of my granddad who died this year,' or 'I felt sad as well as happy'. It is a safe place and time for them to bring such memories – though the adult who is helping them walk the spiral will need to be aware of, and comfortable with, the possibility that it may evoke sadness as well as joy.

The ending of the spiral is as important as any other part. I tell the children that their happy memories are like candles that burn inside them and never go out, but that now I am going to do some 'magic' with their actual candle. I use a candle snuffer and go slowly round the circle of lights snuffing each one by holding the snuffer over the tea light and then lifting it with a flourish, allowing the smoke to spiral upwards towards the ceiling. It was a particular pleasure to have one streetwise Year 6 boy, familiar with all the latest technology of the 21st century, respond to a simple candle snuffer with a look of awe and the single word, 'Cool!'

When I put out their candles I place my hand gently on their shoulder – that is the time when if they wish they can share what the spiral meant to them - and they often do, though I do not invite it.

Whatever they share, whether it is a memory, a smile or simply silence, it is accepted quietly.

Strengths Builders that children can do on their own might include keeping a 'Happy Memory' album or starting a journal that focuses primarily, though not exclusively, on the good things that happen to them. Also being aware of their own top strengths and trying to use them in new ways can increase both happiness and hopefulness.

Spirituality

The *Spiral* walk builds hope, certainly and it is also a key Strengths Builder for spirituality. During the spiral I have seen children's faces shine with a simple joy and wonder. Since introducing the spiral, I have realised that in every class one or two children show by their reactions that this, for them, is simply wonderful. I have concluded that these are children for whom spirituality is a top strength. We do not always have much time for spiritual reflection in our crowded school days, but for all of us, and especially for such children, it is an important part of an emotionally healthy life.

Spirituality is an awareness of and belief in a non material aspect of life. It may take the form of traditional religious belief and practice but increasingly there are people outside orthodox religion who would identify themselves as 'spiritual'. Spirituality implies a belief in something beyond the self and the immediate group, something that provides meaning to life and a link to morality and goodness. That something may be God or a sense of the divine, it might be a sense of purpose in life, a belief in justice or the importance of gratitude, or a belief in peace or education.

Involvement in religious practice is associated in young people with less anti social behaviour and more academic success. Religious or spiritual beliefs and practice are also associated with better physical and psychological health. They are linked to a range of virtues, such as forgiveness, hope, kindness and compassion.

Spiritual awareness in its broadest sense, an ability to think deeply about life and its meaning, is an important part of healthy emotional growth. Besides the *Spiral,* which is perhaps the most overtly spiritual of all the Strengths Builders, there are others which contribute to this reflective, thoughtful aspect of life. All of the meditations cultivate spiritual awareness. So do the Strengths Builders like *Pearls* and *WWW* that encourage positive reflection and the cultivation of hope. Hope, gratitude and love of beauty are all closely linked with spirituality, so Strengths Builders used for these strengths may also be used for encouraging and exercising spirituality.

One - often overlooked - aspect of spirituality is, in my opinion, cooking and in particular, baking. For me, baking, making bread or cakes, is fundamentally an act of love. Making *Christmas cakes* as a gift for someone builds on this characteristic and adds to it another important aspect of spirituality, waiting. A Christmas cake takes time, you first make the cake, then you add brandy for a week or so and then marzipan and finally icing and then you wait a little more until Christmas day and you eat it. What could be more spiritual than that? Consider letting all the children make individual Christmas cakes through the Advent festival.

Stories that encourage spirituality include the many sacred stories of the world's faith traditions. If you are having a predominantly Christian Advent festival, you can use the traditional Christmas story. It is very effective told in assemblies gradually over the weeks of Advent, introducing the characters one at a time and lighting a candle on an Advent wreath for each one. I have told it as *The Road to Bethlehem* and literally built a road of pebbles that lengthens each week as another character is introduced. I include this version of the Christmas story at the end of this chapter.

Individual Strengths Builders for spirituality might include spending time alone, meditating or praying, finding out about another faith tradition, learning a prayer by heart and using it, reading a religious book. There are some lovely web sites for older children to use. One of my favourites is **www.gratefulness.org** where you can literally 'light a candle' as a prayer or positive thought for another person – children would love the opportunity to do this.

Humour

Humour is included in Peterson and Seligman's list of 'transcendent' strengths because it takes individuals out of themselves and may help to deal with adversity by finding the incongruity, the ridiculousness of a situation. Humour, as opposed to wit or sarcasm, is benevolent, and implies a sympathetic heart.

Humour has different aspects. Telling jokes is one but a person may be humorous and never tell jokes. It also includes making people smile or laugh, an ability to see the light side of a situation and a playful enjoyment of life.

Though there is no long term evidence for the health benefits of humour, laughter is certainly good for us, having a positive effect on mood and on our bodies. A good sense of humour may be a defining feature of good mental health. It is suggested that humour may be developed by encouraging a playful attitude to life. The ability to create humour is associated with creativity and intelligence.

Teachers need to be aware of the negative aspects and uses of humour. My own way of dealing with unkind laughter is to label it for what it is, unkindness. Genuine humour is constructive, not destructive, it builds social relationships and makes people feel better, not worse, about themselves. The litmus test, for me, of humour, is 'Does this hurt someone?'

Some traditional stories are based on a sense of the ridiculous. *Lazy Jack*, where a boy tries to carry out his mother's instructions to the letter and ends up giving a donkey a lift home on his shoulders, is one such story, but you will find others, equally silly. Researching, collecting and telling *Funny Stories* would be an appropriate Strengths Builder for a class of older children or teenagers.

Other Strengths Builders would be a *Joke Book Competition*. Telling jokes is really another kind of story telling – good jokes are just short, funny stories. What is the difference between telling jokes and telling stories? All good jokes are stories, but not all good stories are jokes. Learning and telling jokes, collecting them in a book and awarding prizes for best (or worst) jokes would be a good thing to do at a dark time of year.

Since playfulness may encourage the development of humour, any playful activity might be included as a Strengths Builder for humour. Consider how to encourage a playful attitude to lessons among older children and teenagers. The use of games, comedy clips, music and funny illustrations would all be of use in this respect.

The Road to Bethlehem

Isaiah

Advent is a time for getting ready for the mystery of Christmas, for travelling together along the road to Bethlehem. The first person we meet is a man called Isaiah. Isaiah lived long ago. Long before Christmas was invented. And Isaiah was called a prophet, a person who listens and sees clearly what is happening around him and who reminds people of what is important in life. Isaiah listened to his people, the Israelites. He listened to the darkness, to the wars and the troubles of his own day – long, long ago. Above all, Isaiah listened to God.

And Isaiah looked back and remembered. He remembered a time when all his people had listened to God as carefully as he did. And Isaiah looked forward with hope. He was hoping for a time when someone would be born who would teach all people to live in peace. He is seen as someone who, many years before the birth of Jesus Christ, saw that it was going to happen. And these are some words of Isaiah that have come down to us from thousands and thousands of years ago. Isaiah said, 'The people who walked in darkness have seen a great light; those who lived in a land of deep darkness – on them light has shined.' (This is Isaiah's candle, which will light the road to Bethlehem...)

Mary and Joseph

Further along the road we meet Mary and Joseph travelling to Bethlehem.

Mary was a girl who looked back and remembered. She remembered an angel coming to her. These are the words of the angel, it said, 'Do not be afraid, Mary...you will become pregnant and give birth to a son and you will name him Jesus. He will be great and will be called the Son of the Most High God.' And Mary looked forward with hope. She was hoping that her baby would be born in safety. (Here is Isaiah's candle and here is Mary's candle to light the road to Bethlehem...)

The Shepherds

Here are some shepherds, travelling to Bethlehem. These shepherds looked back and remembered seeing angels in the sky above them, shining with a great light and singing, 'Glory to God in the highest heaven, and peace to his people on earth.' And they were looking forward, hoping to see a baby, lying in a manger, somewhere in Bethlehem. (Here is Isaiah's candle and here is Mary's candle and here is the shepherds' candle to light the way to Bethlehem…)

The Wise Men

The Wise Men travelled from a land far, far away to reach Bethlehem. They looked back and remembered a new star appearing in the night sky and setting out to follow it, asking wherever they went, 'Where is the baby born to be the king of the Jews? We saw his star when it came up in the east and we have come to worship him.' They are looking forward, hoping to find the new born king and to give him gifts. (Here is Isaiah's candle and here is Mary's candle and here is the shepherds' candle, and here is the Wise Men's candle to light the way to Bethlehem…)

The Christ Child

Soon it will be Christmas Day, and here, at the end of the road, is the Christ Child, lying in the manger. And we can bring to him our memories, the things we look back on, and our hopes because he was born to share in them. We can travel to Bethlehem and bring our memories and our hopes to the Christ Child.

(Here is Isaiah's candle and here is Mary's candle and here is the shepherds' candle, and here is the Wise Men's candle and here is the Christ candle, to light the way to Bethlehem…)

The children can walk the road you have built and leave Christmas wishes and / or happy memories by the manger.

TWELVE

Performing Arts

THE PERIOD AFTER CHRISTMAS can be a difficult time of year. We are often tired, because of the Christmas preparations and festivities, and it is cold and dark outside. Spring seems a long way away. We need courage, sometimes, just to get out of bed in the mornings and perseverance to keep going until the spring flowers and sunshine arrive to cheer us. These two strengths, courage and perseverance, or persistence, seem appropriate ones to focus on at this time of year

I have also suggested a focus on love of beauty. This is partly because there is beauty in the natural world in January and February but it is harder to find, so looking for it can lift our spirits. It is also because it seems a good idea to bring beauty inside at this time of year, to fill homes, workplaces and schools with colour and music and works of art to lift spirits and inspire us to carry on.

Holding a performing arts festival is one way to draw these strengths together and a way of brightening up the term. The Society for Storytelling (**www.sfs.org.uk**) holds a National Storytelling Week in the UK in the first week of February each year. Your school might want to hold events that link in with this national event. Storytelling is an excellent performing art to work on with children. Alternatively, if your school community has a particular talent for dance, or drama, or music, you might focus on them instead.

This festival does not have to be about performing arts, however. It is really intended to celebrate what your school does best, to spend time enjoying your particular strengths and telling the world about them. The first school I worked with on a festival programme was particularly strong in the performing arts, so that was what they chose. If you are good at science, hold a science festival. You will find many ways of encouraging persistence, courage and love of beauty through science because you will naturally think in scientific terms and language. If history is something that lots of staff love, hold a history fortnight, with pageants and reconstructions and displays – again, you will find plenty of scope for building the key strengths for this time of year. One school I work with is very strong at visual arts so this is the time of year they focus particularly on their favourite artists, producing and displaying stunning art work and celebrating what they are good at. Design and enjoy your own festival – what are you best at? Celebrate it.

I have used a variety of stories for this festival. You might use traditional tales like *The Billy Goats Gruff* for younger children – it is a tale that contains courage, but they can also exercise courage in telling it for themselves. Older children and teenagers enjoy lesser known legends and myths and I include one, Where is the Moon? at the end of the chapter. It is a mixture of two Lincolnshire legends retold with an emphasis on persistence. Many stories contain beauty – favourites of mine are the Scottish creation myths such as *Beira Queen of Winter*, a story I heard first on Orkney from story teller Lynn Barbour.

Courage or Bravery

Perhaps the most important thing to understand about courage is that it does not imply an absence of fear, in fact quite the reverse. Courage is for when we do feel afraid but need to act – if we are not frightened, we do not need courage. Brave people are those who face their fears and overcome them, not letting fear prevent them from doing what is right or what they need to do.

Some writers describe courage as a higher order strength – it is the strength that enables us to use all the other strengths as much as we can. We need courage to persevere in the face of difficulties, we need courage to form close, intimate, loving relationships because intimacy makes us vulnerable. We need courage to grow and develop because we must take risks to do so. In Chinese philosophy, courage is the quality required to stay true to values such as kindness and truthfulness.

Courage is also essential for learning. Not understanding something is naturally a scary sensation – it produces feelings of vulnerability and anxiety – will I master this, will someone laugh at me/shout at me for not understanding or making a mistake? Sometimes highly anxious children find learning difficult, precisely because they cannot cope with the natural fear that they feel for long enough to master the new skill or area of knowledge. They reject learning as 'boring' when what they actually mean is 'too frightening,' thinking that they may not be able to cope.

As I have said before, using courage builds true self esteem. Going outside our comfort zones and surviving helps us feel good about ourselves and builds the confidence that we will survive the next challenge, too.

Children tend to think of courage in quite physical (and often male) terms – soldiers are brave, physical dangers are frightening. However, one of the most common fears among adults is public speaking, which involves overcoming the fear of ridicule. It is equally common among children. Often the best way of building courage is just by doing what we are scared of – we grow courage, like a muscle, by using it. We learn we can survive in our stretch zones by surviving – so we can build the confidence to try it again.

There is also the quiet courage of endurance, which some children show by surviving in circumstances that would appal us. A simple, 'I think you show great courage sometimes' may mean the world to such children.

Courage can be promoted by practice – giving children the opportunities to exercise it. *Philosophy* is a Strengths Builder that will provide ample opportunities to practice courage – it can take courage just to speak in front of peers, courage to disagree or to be disagreed with, courage to express an unpopular opinion. *Story Telling* will also provide ample opportunities for confronting the fear of public speaking. *Opinion Lines* can be used as a Strengths Builder for courage – emphasise the need to decide on an opinion that is theirs, not their best friend's, and point out how brave we need to be to disagree with lots of people.

Any activity that asks children to choose, publicly, can give an opportunity to exercise courage. *Choose a Story* is another example. Have cards ready with some favourite stories written on them. Let the children choose by placing stars or stickers on the one they want to hear the most. Let them do this one by one, so that each choice is thoughtful, deliberate and public, and emphasise that this is their choice. Discourage comment from the onlookers, as cheers and other exclamations can make courageous, individual choice difficult.

You then exercise courage by being prepared to tell any one of the stories they have chosen, immediately and without revision! Modelling is another important way of promoting courage. You do this when you tell stories and when, in your teaching, you move outside your own comfort zone.

The encouragement of our group is also a factor that helps us develop our own courage. Fostering an encouraging atmosphere, even very specifically teaching *Encouragement* as a Strengths Builder and skill, will help to build cohesion and group spirit in your class – they should all be helping and encouraging each other, not competing and putting each other down, as is too often the case. What does *Encouragement* look and sound like – what words might you use, what actions, to encourage somebody else to do their best? Can you even raise the status of 'class encourager' and make it a title they compete to achieve? A Strengths Builders like *Speakers and Listeners* also works very directly on the social skills that form the basis of positive encouraging relationships.

Speakers and Listeners is a game based on the listening training that is done on counselling courses. Children work in pairs, with one being the speaker and the other the listener. The speaker goes first and talks for one minute about – anything really. What they like to do at the weekend, their last holiday, what they feel grateful about in life. I tend to keep to positive subjects. The listener needs to listen – with their head, with their eyes and with their face. *Listening with your head* means concentrating on what you hear and remembering it. *Listening with your eyes* means looking at the speaker all the time. *Listening with your face* means reflecting what you hear and see – smile if they smile, look sad if they look sad. When the speaker has finished the listener feeds back what they heard – to prove they were listening with their head. Then the speaker marks their listener on how they listened – they get one mark for each way that they listened:

- With their head (i.e., they remembered what was said) - one mark
- With their eyes (i.e., they kept looking) - one mark
- With their face (i.e., they reflected the feelings of the speaker) - one mark

One out of three makes you an OK listener, two marks make you a GOOD listener, and three marks a VERY GOOD listener. Only the listener knows what mark they get. Then the process is reversed.

Done occasionally, and with children rotated so they get a turn to work with everyone in the class, this Strengths Builder will build courage (good listening takes courage and so does talking to someone who isn't a close friend). It will also teach the basics of good listening and create a good sense of community within the classroom. The class is a team – they *should* be encouraging each other and helping each other to learn but all too often, classes behave as though they are in competition with each other and sometimes are just plain horrid to each other and to you. Don't tolerate it! Real courage is the courage to be kind and to *encourage* one another.

Specific stories that reflect the strength of courage are those that involve quests, facing and overcoming dangers. *The Three Billy Goats Gruff* does this well for young children – all the goats feel fear as they cross the bridge – but they do it anyway. For older children or teenagers, some of the hero myths might be good to tell in this context. Conall is a Scottish hero whose story I have used; you might research Greek stories such as *Hercules* or look at simple English tales like *Jack the Giant Killer*.

Individual Strengths Builders children can use if they want to work on their courage might include suggestions like 'Make a new friend' since talking to people we don't know well requires courage. Older pupils might research great acts of courage, looking at recent heroes like the fire fighters who died saving others on 9/11.

Persistence

There is little success without persistence. It is the key to academic success and often to success in life. It is not a universal good, however. Sometimes our goals are unobtainable and giving up is the right thing to do – success and happiness really depend on knowing when to persist and when to give up.

Persistence is closely linked to courage but it is not usually fear that leads to lack of persistence, but boredom or the desire to do something else more interesting. Self control is an important element in persistence so Strengths Builders that encourage self control, like *Meditation* and *Create a Story Space*, described later in the chapter, may also be used to build persistence. Fear of looking foolish can contribute to a lack of persistence. Studies show that we will actually persist longer at tasks that are perceived as difficult because if we fail there is less of a blow to our self esteem than if we fail at something perceived as easy.

Persistence has been shown to be linked to explanatory style and to optimism. If you typically expect bad things to happen, you are simply more likely to give up, while if you tend to expect success you will persist longer in the face of setbacks. For these reasons, Strengths Builders like *Eeyore Thinking* and *WWW* would be useful to use for building persistence as well as hope. Persistence is also more likely if we are cheerful, so using a Strengths Builder like *Mood Booster* or *Treasure Chest* to prepare for learning may be helpful.

Persistence can be encouraged and, once more, it is praising **effort** that achieves this. Studies showed that praising children as intelligent after a failure *decreased* their persistence whereas praising their effort increased it. Learning to blame failure on lack of effort rather than lack of ability is also important. Girls are particularly prone to blame failure on low ability so helping them to transfer that blame onto low effort is an important strategy for teachers. We can do little about our 'intelligence' at any given moment, but our effort is within our control.

We have known for a long time that negative labelling is harmful – telling a child they are 'naughty' or 'not very bright'. It is now thought that positive labelling, telling a child they are intelligent as in the research above, may be just as problematic. It is worth thinking about this when we are noticing strengths. If we tell a child, 'You are kind' we label them. The child knows that they are not always kind or don't always feel kind, and so the label both fails to describe who they really are deep down and implies that this is how they must always be. To say, 'That was a kind thing to do' is both more accurate and more affirming. Labelling behaviour, whether positive or negative, seems more helpful than labelling the person. For example 'You really stuck at that,' 'That was a brave thing to do,' or 'I'm impressed by the way you always notice beautiful things' all say more about the behaviour, rather than being about the person.

Persistence is also encouraged by good relationships and social support. A teacher can do little about their pupil's support networks outside school. Much can be done, however, to build supportive relationships in the classroom. If everyone is rooting for you, you are much more likely to keep going when the going gets tough. One Strengths Builder that can help to do this is *Strengths Spotting*. This can be done in different ways but one that I have used effectively to build better relationships between peers is to make strengths posters, where children work in groups with people they would not usually choose to work with and help one another to identify their top strengths. They put their names on the poster and then simply decorate it with their top strengths, using words and images. This leads to more positive conversations than often happen with some of the children we teach. The children can either make a poster each or a composite one for the whole group but either way, they work with peers to determine their top strengths.

Classrooms should operate as teams where one person's success reflects glory on everyone, it does not diminish them. Learning to celebrate successes – other people's as well as your own - may well be the key to getting more of them.

Again, how we view failure is an important element in whether or not we persist at a task. If failure equates to disaster, we may give up early rather than risk any more. However, the most successful soldiers, artists and scientists in history have been those with the most failures – because they took the attitude that here was an experience from which they could learn.

Story Telling is a great Strengths Builder for persistence – to master a story you have to practice, it is as simple as that! Some stories also contain positive messages about persistence, and you can tell these stories to indirectly reinforce this strength. They show persistence in action. Stories like that of St Brendan, who sailed the oceans for years until he found America, or the Lincolnshire story, *Where is the Moon*, which I retell at the end of the chapter with a particular emphasis on persistence.

If you choose to focus on story telling during this festival, learning stories to tell to other children, either in small groups or even in assembly, provides opportunities for children to build both courage and persistence at the same time. Assemblies can become an important element of a performing arts festival, since they are the goal the children can work towards.

There are films that echo the importance of persistence too. One of my favourites is *Finding Nemo*, a tale of amazing persistence on the part of a fish – and very funny too. When I tell younger children about persistence I remind them of Dory, the blue fish in the film who has short term memory loss. She tells Nemo's dad, when he is feeling discouraged, to sing to himself 'Just keep swimming, just keep swimming.' I use the BSL sign for persistence, one hand chopping down on the side of the other hand and wiggle my hips and sing to them, 'Just keep trying, just keep trying.' I inform the startled teachers that they are to do the same to encourage the children in their class. The children love it, and persistence has consequently become a favourite strength!

Individual Strengths Builders the children can use might include 'Where There's a Will,' which involves them setting themselves a goal and working out how they are going to achieve it, then carrying on until they do. Another would be a personal *Treasure Chest* or a simple photo album of happy memories, since looking at it may well provide the mood boost necessary to stick at a task.

Love of Beauty

Love or appreciation of excellence and beauty is one of Peterson and Seligman's 'transcendent' strengths – strengths that connect us with something greater than ourselves. It is associated with emotions of awe and wonder and may be felt in response to great art, or music, or drama, but also in response to excellence in other fields, for example, in football, or in science, or in the realms of moral goodness – we may be moved to tears by kindness or by courage. An absence of this strength may result in a blinkered attitude to all that is beautiful or moving, and a cynical approach to life.

Little is really known about how to build this strength but the assumption is that being raised in an environment where beauty and excellence are noticed and valued may help children to develop this trait for themselves. *Strengths Spotting* may be used to encourage this strength too, since it helps children to focus on what is good in their peers, building positive mental pathways as they do so. The *Atelier* System from Italy might also be incorporated into the curriculum as a Strengths Builder for love of beauty, since it allows children to play with

and create beautiful works of art in a supportive and playful environment. I have used the Scottish creation myth *Beira, Queen of Winter* to
foster a love of beauty. Films to watch might include *Billy Elliot*, a story
of courage in the pursuit of an ideal.

A key Strengths Builder I would recommend for all the strengths
of this festival is *Create a Story Space*. It requires a calm and self
controlled approach to story telling which supports persistence. It
requires courage of the children since at different points they become
the centre of attention. It allows them to work together to create something beautiful.

Create a Story Space

This Strengths Builder developed from my use of props to help
children begin to work creatively with stories. I avoided using the hall
in schools because it is hard to create the right intimate atmosphere for
story telling. Then I spotted some inexpensive rugs, just right for two
children to work on, which I realised could be used to create a 'space
within a space' and to open up the possibility of working in a school
hall. It allows the class to take charge, for themselves, of creating the
right visual and emotional atmosphere for story telling, exercising
autonomy, courage and considerable self control as they do so, and
creating something beautiful together.

The activity has a meditative start and finish – with lots of buzz
and noise in the middle - and it may encourage flow and creativity. At
the same time the children are learning to take charge of the story chest
for themselves, to be independent and resourceful and to exercise
choice and decision making, important features in building optimism
and self esteem.

The activity happens in the hall or other large space, but begins in the classroom with a story and requires two adults for it work at its best. Before the session begins, place a story chest and a pile of at least 15 rugs in the centre of the hall.

Tell the children a story and then explain that to work creatively themselves, in story telling or making a picture from a story, they need first to create the right atmosphere, the right 'environment,' and that they can do this by working together. First, they play a 'self control game' that involves them walking, slowly and in silence, alone to the hall. They must watch the adult who remains in the classroom who will nod at them when it is their turn to move. Then they are to get up and walk calmly and sensibly to the hall where they are to join you in making one large circle. You go first, standing, looking at them and then going out slowly and deliberately.

You enter the hall and sit to one side facing the door. Gesture and smile at the first child who enters and point to the space next to you. They should come and sit next to you, about a metre away, the next child next to them and so on until all the children have entered and are sitting in a large circle.

Ask the two children next to you to stand, walk to the middle, pick up a rug and together bring it back to their place, spread it out and sit on it. As they are returning, gesture to the next pair to stand and fetch their rug, and then the next pair until everyone is sitting on a rug, including you if possible. Some of the time let the children work in silence, in between, in a quiet calm voice make comments such as 'I love the fact that you are all waiting so patiently for one another, that's really kind and excellent teamwork;' 'You moved really calmly and gracefully Robert, well done;' 'The silence is wonderful, you all have such good self control;' 'Well done for being ready, you two, you were really paying attention'. Your slow, positive reinforcement will focus the children's attention on what you are looking to encourage, and your calm, quiet voice will help to create a relaxed, thoughtful atmosphere for them to work in, and will help the children relax, too.

When all the rugs are out the same process continues, either individually this time or again in pairs, for unpacking the chest. You will need to direct them the first few times. Basically each child gets out one item, but depending on the number of children in the class, the pile of story bags can count as one item or two, the story cloths as one item or two and the scarves as one item or 12 separate ones – each child needs to get out at least one thing. Once you have worked this out, use the same procedure for subsequent sessions and the children will soon need no direction, they will remember how to do it. The children are to move to the centre as the previous child or pair of children is returning to their rug. They should be watching and paying attention the whole time so they see what is happening and when it is their turn. In this way you are building focus and concentration as well as a relaxing and peaceful atmosphere.

The first child opens the chest, the second spreads a beautiful cloth out, then each subsequent child gets out one thing and decides where on the cloth to arrange it. You will be encouraging them to move slowly, carefully, to choose where to place each item so that we create a beautiful arrangement, to show the other children what it is they are getting out, to be brave because they are the centre of attention, to notice when it is their turn to stand and so on, in effect giving a quiet commentary that helps build atmosphere and provide positive encouragement and feedback.

The child who finds the chest empty closes it and then you are ready to begin. First comment on their teamwork and the work of art they have already produced – you may wish to photograph it to look at later – and commend the quiet atmosphere which each of them has helped to build. Then decide how they are to choose props. For the younger children, you can walk round the circle and let them know that you will nod at each one when it is their turn to get up and choose, for example, three billy goats or something to be a brick house. You can keep careful control in this way of how many children are in the centre choosing at any one time. For older ones, I have just said that one of you needs to stay on your mat while the other goes to choose, so talk together first about what you will need, and work together and take turns to go and collect what you wish to use.

When all the choices are made the children can spread a story cloth on their mat and start working together as you wish – retelling the story or making a scene or character from it or just 'playing with it' – this kind of free symbolic play has immense value throughout the primary years for building creativity, emotional awareness and control, empathy, resilience and optimism. You can never really let children do too much of it. Never worry that they are 'just playing' - it is so important and so frequently overlooked.

If you have asked the children to tell the story they have heard or another, move round and listen. I have found that if I keep my gaze down and my ear obviously turned to them, even children who hadn't been story telling will start! If I look at them they turn and talk to me rather than continuing to work together.

Again, you might use a digital camera to record the work and follow it up later in class. They will be able to explain to everyone else which story they were working on and what their props represented, hence extending the speaking and listening element of the lesson.

The end of the session is as important as the beginning, so try to leave at least 15 minutes initially to tidy away (it should get quicker as the children grow used to the activity but don't rush it – learning not to rush is something we all need to work on!). First, the children need to put the props back in their boxes and bags on the central cloth, restoring it to its former beauty. Then they pack the chest in exactly the same way that they unpacked it, one by one, each following person moving to the middle as the former returns, and noticing for themselves when it is their turn. When the chest is full and the final child has shut it again, the rugs are put away, again in silence and two by two, and the children can return as they came, in stillness to the classroom. Then, the lesson is complete.

Where is the Moon?

I heard this story from an old man who heard it from his granny and so I'm telling it to you. Long ago, but not very far from here, the land was covered by bogs and marshes – great pools of black water, little streams of green water, squishy muddy ditches of brown, smelly water. When the moon shone brightly it was safe to walk among the pools without falling in.

But when there was no moon – for this was long ago before roads or street lights were invented – and darkness covered the bogs and the marshes, then the Bad Things came out of their holes– the quicks and the witches, the bogles and the boggarts and they would poke and prod and push travellers until they tripped and fell into the great pools of black water, or the little streams of green water, or the squishy muddy ditches of brown smelly water. And when the kindly moon heard of this, she decided to come down and see for herself.

And so at the end of the month the moon stepped down and wrapped herself in a great black cloak and covered the shining bright-ness of her hair with a great black hood so that only a tiddy glimmer of light shone from where her toes peeped out at the bottom. And she walked around the bogs and the marshes in between the great pools of black water, past the little streams of green water, and over the squishy muddy ditches of brown, smelly water. But as she walked her great black robe snagged on a twisted branch and she was stuck fast, unable to move. As she struggled to try and free herself the moon heard a man moaning and crying.

It was a traveller and the quicks and the witches, the boggles and the boggarts were poking and prodding and pushing him closer and closer to a great pool of black water, the deepest and darkest pool in the whole marsh. The moon was horrified – she wanted to help the poor traveller – so she kept on struggling and pulling at her cloak to try and free herself. At last she gave such a powerful tug that her hood fell back from the shining brightness of her hair and the marsh was filled with moonlight so bright it felt like day.

The traveller gave a shout of relief and he hurried safely round the black pool and out of the marshes. But the quicks and the witches, the boggles and the boggarts who hate the light of the sun and the light of the moon screamed and scurried and scuttled back into their deep dark holes in the ground.

The traveller was safe but the poor moon was still stuck on that twisted branch and as she pulled and struggled some more her hood fell back over her head and covered her golden hair and darkness covered the marshes once more.

Of course, in the darkness, the quicks and the witches, the boggles and the boggarts could come out and out they came, scurrying and scuttling and squealing with glee. And this time it was the poor moon that they poked and prodded and pushed right into that deep, dark pool of black water and they poked and prodded and pushed her right down to the bottom of that pool and they covered her with a huge stone so that the poor moon was trapped and darkness covered the marshes – in fact, there was just a tiddy glimmer of light were the moon's toes peeped out from the bottom of her cloak, to show that she was there at all.

And there the moon stayed and in the dark nights that followed no one dared go out, only the quicks and the witches and the boggles and the boggarts scurried and scuttled about happily in the darkness.

But the quicks and the witches, the boggles and the boggarts were not the only creatures who lived in the marshes and the bogs. There was also the Tiddy Mun, a little man who never said much but who would help the people who lived there when he could. And so the frightened people called on the Tiddy Mun. The Tiddy Mun never said much but he nodded and started to search for the moon, and the people, though they were frightened of the darkness, searched with him.

Days passed and every night the Tiddy Mun and the people looked for the moon in all the great pools of black water. But they couldn't find her.

Weeks passed and every night the Tiddy Mun and the people looked for the moon in every single little stream of green water. But they couldn't find her.

Months passed and every night the Tiddy Mun and the people looked for the moon in all the squishy muddy ditches of brown smelly water. But they couldn't find her.

In fact, the Tiddy Mun and the people kept on looking night after night after night. At last a traveller remembered seeing a great light shining near the biggest, darkest, deepest pool in the whole marsh and he told the Tiddy Mun and the people. The Tiddy Mun never said much but he nodded and led the people to the pool and there he noticed a tiddy glimmer of light shining up from under a stone at the bottom of that deep, dark pool and he pointed down into the water.

The people fetched ropes and said their prayers – because the quicks and the witches, the boggles and the boggarts were crowding around them. The Tiddy Mun tied the ropes around the stone, and then he and the people started to pull. They pulled and they pulled though the quicks and the witches screamed at them. They pulled and they pulled though the boggles and boggarts poked at them. They pulled and they pulled nearly the whole night long until at last the stone moved.

There was a sudden splash and a burst of dazzling moonlight shot up out of the water and there was the moon, shining in the sky once more, flooding the marshes with brightness and driving the quicks and the witches, the boggles and the boggarts scurrying and scuttling back into their holes.

The Tiddy Mun looked up at the kindly moon and raised his hat in greeting and someone says, though I don't know if it's true, that the moon waved back and she smiled too.

THIRTEEN

Easter: A Celebration of Love, Kindness and Friendship

T HE EASTER STORY, unlike the Christmas Story, is one which many schools and teachers feel uncomfortable about addressing, let alone celebrating. Christmas, of course, is the story of a baby, the baby Jesus. The adult Jesus is rather more challenging and the story of Easter contains both a cruel death and an event, the resurrection, in which we may or may not believe.

However, it is the most amazing story and one which underpins much of the art, literature and music of the Western world. And it is a story that contains all of the strengths necessary for forming close loving relationships and a positive view of the world: love, kindness and friendship. So, do we avoid the Easter story because it contains a death and a supernatural event? Or do we value and celebrate it as the core story of the Christian faith?

Death is a part of life and cruelty happens. The subjects we avoid in the classroom are those that children may feel most anxious about. Our avoidance is obvious to children and it says to them, very clearly, that these subjects are so terrible that we, as adults, cannot bear to put them into words, let alone think about them. Stories, both sacred and secular, provide a perfect vehicle for dealing with difficult subjects, like death and cruelty, in a safe and contained way.

I would not instigate a discussion of death and bereavement in the classroom – they are powerful subjects and can arouse very powerful emotions. And it is a classroom, not a therapy session. If children raise these topics themselves because of something they have seen or heard, I would always respond honestly and to the best of my ability, but I would never take 'death' as a suitable subject for discussion. On the other hand, I do tell stories that contain death and I do leave the death in. The Easter story contains a death – it is immensely sad and moving. I can cope with that and because I can cope with it, so can the children. Stories provide a way of thinking about death at second hand – we are thinking of someone else's sadness and loss, not our own. We feel a little of the emotion involved, but only a little. Like a pressure cooker, listening to a sad story allows a little of our own stored up sadness to escape. If I am asked to tell you about my own sadness, it may open a floodgate which the classroom is not meant to witness or contain.

So tell the Easter story, but tell it quietly and with restraint, and put the death of Jesus in the context of his amazing, love filled life. When we tell the Easter story as the central story of this festival, we model it on *The Road to Bethlehem* and it becomes *The Road to Jerusalem*. It is a parallel but different journey, and the road is once again built in the hall over the weeks before Easter, using pebbles. We think about the different things Jesus did in his life and in holy week and we make links with the children's own experiences. We remember Jesus the story teller who told stories about kindness – and we think about people who show us kindness; we look at Jesus the healer who loved people and made them better and we think of people we know who are sick; we think in turn of Jesus the miracle worker who calmed a storm, Jesus entering Jerusalem on a donkey while the crowds cheered, Jesus eating with his friends, and Jesus dying on a cross.

All of these can form separate assemblies, part of the lengthening road to Jerusalem. The last one is sad and is told with the lights out. Children can survive sadness. However, the final assembly, which we time for the last day and often just a few hours after the assembly about Jesus' death, tells the Christian story of the resurrection. We fill the hall with lights and flowers and the children travel the road to Jerusalem themselves, keeping Jesus Christ company on his journey. The children might receive chocolate eggs as they reach the end of the road or, as one school did, they may help to decorate the road with ribbons and beads, and to transform it from a place of pain into a work of art.

Do you need to believe in the resurrection to hold this assembly – do you need to be a Christian? I would say not. If you believe that love is stronger than death, and that good can arise from the most painful of situations, then these themes are at heart what this story is about, and you can tell it with integrity. It is the story that Christians tell. A person of any faith, or a person of no faith can respect the love and the hope that is at its core.

Christianity, of course, does not have a monopoly on stories about love and kindness. I include at the end of this chapter a Buddhist story about great love. It is actually a story about one of the incarnations of the Buddha. Buddhists believe he was reborn in animal form many times to help all creatures. This is a story of one of those incarnations.

The story of Guru Nanak, descending into a river for three days and arising to tell the world about the love of God is one in which I personally find many parallels with Christianity. Again, it is a wonderful story to tell.

One important feature of work on strengths and positive emotions, it seems to me, is to find space for uncomfortable emotions and sadness. It is possible that an over emphasis on social and emotional learning may be as bad as too little, and that too much focus on teamwork and on feeling positive may disadvantage depressed students, stifling healthy scepticism and debate.

Using traditional stories should certainly help address this concern. They are full of scepticism and cunning and rebellion, as well as morality and co-operation, and they make important space for sadness and despair alongside joy and triumph. Personally, if I am doing a lot of work on love and kindness and friendship I throw in a few traditional tales that allow my vengeful, aggressive side to breath! It is important to provide balance and traditional stories do this beauti-fully.

Love

Love has fascinated humankind for thousands of years. In the past few decades psychologists have started to study it scientifically though perhaps there are aspects that will always remain a mystery. I hope so. There are three aspects to love - thought, feelings and actions - and there are three particular kinds of loving relationship – the love of those on whom we depend, our love for those who depend on us, and romantic love, between peers. Relationships can contain more than one kind of love and can change over time. For a relationship to involve love it needs to be within a reciprocal relationship – we may think we 'love' an actor or football team but the feelings run in one direction only, so would not be classed as love.

Love is not just the nature of the bond between parents and chil-dren, or between lovers. There is also the love between team mates, between co-workers, the love we have for mentors or for those who inspire us, and the love between pupil and teacher. I heard, not long ago, a Head Teacher talk of one of his colleague's struggles with a particularly challenging class. This teacher, the head commented, had lost his love for his class and needed to regain it. I thought then what an unusual and brave comment it was – and how true.

We are often unwilling as teachers to admit that our pupils love us – it is indeed a scary responsibility. We are also unwilling to admit that we love them – it is seen as unprofessional. But it is not unprofessional – it is essential. The best teachers are those who love their pupils and who channel that love into their teaching.

Children learn to love by being loved. Ideally, each child we teach would have received sensitive, loving care from a significant adult throughout their infancy. This care would provide a safe haven during distress, a base from which to explore the world and learn new things, a basis for believing that future relationships would be similarly warm and fulfilling, and a confidence that people are reliable.

This is not always the case. Children who have not had an experience of sensitive care in infancy, for whatever reason, are likely to be inhibited in their capacity to learn, to require more discipline and attention, to be impulsive and easily frustrated, and to have poorer relationships with their teachers and with their peers.. They are also more likely to bully and to be bullied.

The good news is that every relationship counts. We cannot change early experiences, but just one thoughtful, sensitive, loving relationship, just one adult who seems to understand us, can cause changes inside the most damaged child. And little changes add up. Loving teachers make a difference to the world and to children. It requires courage and patience – other strengths touched on in this book – but love is at the core of excellent teaching.

What is also hopeful is that sensitivity is a skill that can be learned and taught. Deliberate teaching of social skills, like listening and positive responding, can help children make friends and form good relationships. *Speakers and Listeners*, described in Chapter 12 on Performing Arts, is one Strengths Builder that you can use for this *Brilliant Listening* is another. *Brilliant Listening* builds on *Speakers and Listeners* and teaches a crucial skill for building strong relationships – how to respond to good news. In speakers and listeners, the listener must listen with their head, their eyes and their face, remembering what is said, keeping eye contact and reflecting the emotions of the speaker with their face. *Brilliant Listening* entails another kind of listening – listening with all your enthusiasm.

There are four different ways of responding to good news. Take, for example, the good news, 'I had an amazing time at the park yesterday!' There is what psychologists call the active destructive response and what I call the 'Worried Winnie' response – 'Oh, I hope there was someone else there, parks can be so dangerous, I hope you won't be too tired today, you might have over done it!' This sounds concerned, but is actually subtly undermining. Then there is a passive constructive or the classic English response, 'That's nice dear.' Totally underwhelming! There is also a passive destructive response, a teenaged 'Whatever!' The last response, and the only one of the four responses that builds relationships, is an active constructive, or enthusiastic response – 'That sounds great! What did you do?' This response contains genuine enthusiasm and an open question that gets the speaker to say more.

Teach children open questions before you do this, questions or responses that encourage the speaker to go on, such as 'Tell me more,' 'What happened?' 'And?' And let them know, very explicitly, that this is how you build friendships. Play it as often as you like. It is also brilliant for building relationships between teacher and children too. I use this one all the time. Love involves actions as well as thoughts and feelings and *Brilliant Listening* is a way of showing love in action.

Other Strengths Builders that encourage social skills are those that build self awareness and empathy, like *How Do I Feel?* and *Good Bits / Bad Bits*. *Philosophy* is also excellent for building skill in communication.

It is interesting to consider which stories echo love, and which friendship, and what the differences are between the two. I would encourage children to think about that one because I don't have any convincing answers! Stories I would definitely tell to echo the theme of love would be *The Elephant and His Mother*, *The Road to Jerusalem* and the traditional tale, *Beauty and the Beast*.

Kindness

Kindness, showing care and love towards another person not for what *we* will get out of it but because of what *they* will get out of it, is at the heart of most faith traditions and many value systems. Perhaps we could think about kindness as love in action. It is certainly linked with love and also, I would suggest, with courage. True courage is kind and true kindness may require the exercise of courage. Kindness should not be confused with 'niceness' – we may need to be tough and challenging to really put the needs of the other first. Being 'nice' may just buy us an easy life where what is genuinely good for the other person may require effort and discomfort on our part.

I think of parents who avoid the word 'no' because it feels somehow 'not nice' and certainly requires effort – the kind act is to provide firm boundaries and to weather the storm. Interestingly, the British Sign Language gestures for courage and kindness are very similar – both start with the hands on the heart and for courage you take your hands out in fists, and for kindness, in fists with a thumbs-up sign.

Kindness as a trait may be partly inherited and is linked to many positive outcomes – kind people are often happier and healthier so it is a good habit to acquire. There is a strong link between kindness and mood. Feeling happy or cheerful ourselves is likely to make us more willing to be kind to others. The *Mood Booster* Strengths Builder may be useful here.

There is surprisingly little known about how to encourage the development of kindness. My own sense is that it is best modelled by adults and nurtured by a community that explicitly talks about and values kindness. Some children, I was surprised to learn, do not really know what is meant by 'kind'. That may be because they have not expe- rienced very much of it, but it might equally mean that they have never had their attention drawn to it. Commenting on actions, 'That was a kind thing to do' can give children a much better understanding of what we mean by kindness.

Stories I would tell to encourage kindness include a lovely one from Grimm, called *The Queen Bee,* and a favourite saints legend of mine, the story of St. Werburga who resurrects a goose.

Working on the principle that we learn to be kind by being kind and that you get more of what you focus on, you might use a Strengths Builder called *The Kindness Catcher.* During the day, children and adults write the names of anyone they see being kind (and perhaps what they were doing) on a post it note and put it in a jar. At the end of the day you read out the people who have been caught being kind. This idea came from a wonderful site called **www.actsofkindness.org** and you will find many others there, together with quotes for the wall.

Friendship

Some people have a real talent for friendship. Others have to learn how to make friends and go on learning throughout their life times. This strength is based on a combination of intelligences, personal, social and emotional. Personal intelligence involves understanding one self, one's moods and motivations, one's strengths and weaknesses, and what is required for one's personal well-being. Social intelligence involves understanding relationships and what motivates other people, how groups work, how to persuade people to do something. Emotional intelligence is about identifying emotional states in other people and in oneself, and how to use the emotions to facilitate thinking and behaviour.

If friendship is extended beyond relationships with others to include our relationship with ourselves, it seems an appropriate term to use to refer to these three so-called 'hot' intelligences.

There is little research so far on whether these three intelligences necessarily coincide in one person or what they lead to in life. There is an initial indication that they may decrease problem behaviours but the evidence so far is tentative. There is also little known about how to encourage them. What is undeniable is that learning is an emotional event and that emotions can impede learning. Understanding and acknowledging them personally is going to be useful. Social skills and personal skills, I am convinced, can be learned and can improve our relationships with ourselves and with others. This is therefore a strength worth looking at alongside the others.

How Do I Feel? is a Strengths Builder which will help children consider the fact that they may have emotional states and notice them. What is more important than knowing what we feel, however, is knowing what we can do about it. Noticing the emotional after taste of activities, knowing what leaves us tense and angry, and what leaves us calm and cheerful, is a vital personal management skill. This is a pre-requisite of the *Mood Booster,* which can be used alongside a *Personal Treasure Chest* to give children the tools to manage themselves.

Learning to pay compliments, to say simple positive things to one another, is a skill a depressingly small number of adults possess! We can get better at this ourselves, and teach it to children. Having a *Compliments Chair* is one way to do this. Children (and adults) take a turn to sit in a compliments chair – others say what they are good at. Be careful there are no back handed insults allowed to creep through. 'You're better at maths,' 'Sometimes you behave' and 'Mostly you're in a good mood' translate respectively as 'You're useless at English,' 'You usually mess about,' and 'You are sometimes really bad tempered.' The compliments delivered when someone is in the Compliments Chair are to be real compliments – simple, direct, unqualified by a 'mostly' or a 'sometimes' - and personal. Address them **to** the recipient. 'Connor, I think *you*_do kind things and I like the good ideas you have in class.' That is a compliment. Teach them, encourage them, use them.

Strengths spotting encourages social intelligence – an awareness of what others are like and what motivates them - and personal intelligence too, an awareness of our own strengths, likes and dislikes. Stories often contain elements of friendship and social skills. I like a simplified retelling of the epic of Gilgamesh for friendship – a 4000 year old tale about Gilgamesh's love for his friend, Enkidu. Below, I tell the Buddhist story of *The Elephant and His Mother*, which demonstrates a lot of these strengths.

The Elephant and his Mother – A Buddhist Story

Long ago in the mountains of the Himalayas, beside a shining pool, a baby elephant was born. He was the most beautiful elephant in all the mountains, with pure white skin and tusks the colour of rich cream.

His proud mother would pluck the sweetest leaves and the ripest fruits and give them to him saying, 'First you, then me.' And she would fill her trunk with sparkling water from the pool and spray him all over till he shone. And then they would curl up happily in the cool mud together. In the afternoons the mother elephant would lead him to the shade of a rose apple tree and they would rest through the heat of the day.

The baby elephant grew bigger and stronger and more and more handsome. He was the most handsome elephant in all the mountains with his pure white skin and tusks the colour of rich cream. But as he grew bigger and stronger his mother grew older and weaker and her eyes grew blind. The young elephant would pluck the sweetest leaves and the ripest fruits and give them to her saying, 'First you, then me.' And he would fill his trunk with sparkling water from the pool and spray her all over till she shone. And then they would curl up happily in the cool mud together. In the afternoons he would lead his mother into the shade of the rose apple tree and she would rest while her son wandered with the other elephants.

One day a king was out hunting and he spotted the beautiful white elephant. He wanted to ride on him, so he captured the elephant and took him back to his palace. The king treated the white elephant most kindly, dressing him in gold trimmings and offering him the sweetest leaves and ripest fruits to eat. But the elephant wept and would not eat. After many days the king went to the elephant and asked him why he was so miserable.

'My old blind mother has no one to care for her,' the elephant answered. 'I cannot eat and drink while she has nothing.' The king was amazed. 'Never have I seen such kindness,' he said, 'even among humans. And he ordered that the elephant be set free.

The mother elephant was standing by the pool when she felt cool water trickling down her back. 'Is it raining?' she asked, 'or has my son returned to me?' 'It is your son,' said the elephant gently, and they curled up happily in the cool mud together. In the heat of the afternoon he led his mother elephant to the shade of a rose apple tree to rest and he plucked the sweetest leaves and ripest fruits and gave them to her. 'First you, then me,' he said.

FOURTEEN

Our Community

THIS FESTIVAL HAS GREEN as its key colour because it is timed for the first half of the summer term – a green time of year in nature, as the trees are in full leaf and a time when we need the relaxing, calming influence of green – both indoors and outdoors – as exams and tests are looming!

It is also a time to celebrate community – our own learning community, the wider community of parents and neighbours, our regional community and the broader, global community of which we are part. All of these communities sustain and enrich our lives and deserve to be celebrated. You might have a party during this festival to celebrate your school – no other reason, not a Christmas party or an end of term party, just a party to celebrate the adults and children who work together to make your community all that it is, a 'This is who we are!'

party. You can use it to focus on the many gifts, strengths and enthusiasms that different people bring. Fill the school with green balloons and plants and have a ball – literally. Learn dances and poems, tell stories, invent a school song and sing it lustily. Some light relief after exams or even a *Mood Booster* just before them – remember, happy children perform better in tests!

It is also a time to focus on the wider community, to hold special events to which you invite parents if you don't already, to research and collect local stories, not necessarily traditional stories (though they may be), but real stories of local events and history. It is a good time to focus on local history too, and to invite elderly residents into school to tell children about what the area used to look like and how they lived their lives there.

You can certainly find traditional stories as a way of celebrating your regional community. There is an amazing book called *The Lore of the Land* which collects local stories by county. It was there I found the Lincolnshire Tiddy Mun who features in my version of another Lincolnshire story, *Where is the Moon?* It is a particular pleasure telling children a local story that belongs to *them*, not to me, and to their ancestors or to the ancestors who lived in *their* place. Place is important – we should celebrate it more, and explore it and think about it and value and look after it!

Beyond our region is our nation. Celebrating the nation is beginning to be acceptable again in the UK, after years of being a terribly incorrect thing to do. Now we hear calls for a Britishness day, and even the English are beginning to sit up and say, hang on, what about **our** sense of national pride? Generations of children grew up knowing the stories of our national heroes. As children, whenever we finished a Smartie Packet we punched the bottom out, put it to one eye and said, 'I see no signal!' I could not have told you that this commemorated Nelson's refusal to retreat at the Battle of Copenhagen, but I did know it commemorated his refusal to retreat *somewhere*! It is a simple story, but how many children know it today?

My daughter went to a fancy dress party dressed, intimidatingly, as Boudicca or Boadicea. About 3 of the 20 teenagers there had heard of her, let alone knew she lead the British (Iceni) revolt against the Romans. Nelson and Boudicca were not perfect individuals, but they were great leaders, and we sell our children short by failing to tell their stories, however simply, and to celebrate them. And newcomers to this country, immigrants and children of immigrants (and most of us, some-where, are children of immigrants – I have an ancestor called Israel Lipschutz I am delighted to say) deserve to hear the stories of their new country, too. Tell stories of heroes at this time of year, Elizabeth I at Tilbury, (I have the heart of a king and a king of England too!) and Florence Nightingale, Francis Drake and Harold at Hastings. Stirring stuff! I include a story of an early British leader at the end of this chapter.

And of course, there are stories from the global community. This is a perfect time to celebrate the richness and diversity of other countries and other cultures. If children in your class come from all over the world, now is a good time to celebrate and hear about their home countries. They can hear stories from their new country and tell us stories from the country they were born in – and everyone is richer as a result!

The strengths of this festival are so important for building community, honesty – which builds ties of trust; teamwork – which allows us to live and work together and leadership - vital if communities are to grow and flourish. The stories I mentioned above are all stories of great leaders. Teamwork is something we focus on a great deal in schools nowadays, but we are altogether less comfortable with leadership. There is some sense that it is not quite right to put ourselves forward and say, actually, 'Leadership is one of my strengths – I love exercising it.'

It has even been suggested that there is something of a crisis in leadership in the UK. Parents seem reluctant to exercise leadership in the home – some feel almost as if they have no right to say 'No.' The decline in respect for authority has been accompanied by a feeling that authority is somehow suspect in all its forms. But leadership is essential and some children are natural leaders. I suspect, from my work with children and strengths, that those who are natural leaders are not natural team workers and vice versa. Those who are good at teamwork have many opportunities in our current system to exercise their strength – those whose top strength is leadership have considerably fewer opportunities. Perhaps that is why they disrupt – after all, to be disruptive, you must have leadership potential otherwise everyone would ignore or squash you. We need leaders and we need to let children use their leadership strengths more.

Leadership

Leadership is a disposition to influence and help others, guiding and motivating a group towards a successful outcome. There is some disagreement about whether leadership is a personality trait or is dependent on social circumstances – it is most likely a combination of the two. In my work with children, I find consistently that some children are natural leaders.

To be effective, a leader must have good social skills, self awareness and a genuine desire to use their leadership skills to help others. Someone who is out for glory is not a good leader – they may be effective in the short term, but in terms of genuine leadership we can distinguish between a leader who is interested in themselves first and a leader who wants to serve others.

The world of business works hard to grow good leaders by focussing mostly on particular skills. Alternatively, it is possible to focus more on the qualities of a leader - integrity, reliability, the desire to serve others, self confidence, sociability, self awareness, enjoying the use of power (but for others and not for self), the ability to inspire.

Speakers and Listeners is a good Strengths Builder for leadership, as children tend to be less aware of the need for a leader to listen as much, if not more than, they talk. *Brilliant Listeners* would also be useful. A *Young Leaders Award* could be developed in school and awarded to those who think of a task to help the community, and motivate and direct others to achieve it.

Tell stories of good leaders and encourage children to collect and retell others. Be aware of yourself as a leader and discuss this with children. Notice, with them, the different situations in which they lead – all older children in a school are leaders and should be encouraged to enjoy and use wisely the influence they possess. All children are leaders of themselves – *personal leadership* - and we all need to learn to be good ones.

Teamwork and Citizenship

The other side of leadership is, of course, teamwork. A leader cannot lead unless he has a team or group of which to be the leader. Citizenship is not synonymous with team work but is closely related to it. Teamwork has a focus on the behaviours necessary to get on with others in a group, to collaborate and co-operate while citizenship involves a feeling of loyalty and responsibility to the group and to the common good, above narrow self interest. An individual with these strengths can be relied on to pull their weight, to be loyal, and to work for the good of the group rather than for personal gain.

Responsibility is the natural balance to rights. Politicians in recent years have called for a return to such a balance. The conditions that foster a sense of civic responsibility in young people are a sense that the community respects and listens to them, as well as expecting them to respect and listen to it. They are more likely to identify with a community's goals and to serve it if they feel a sense of being valued by the community and have a say in community affairs. A feeling of being connected to the community makes violation of community norms less likely. School councils are an obvious way to foster this sense of belonging but so are the many individual moments when teachers listen to children, value their opinions, show them respect and actively intervene to stop bullying and exclusion.

There is a downside to a strong sense of identity with a group. That is when it encourages the exclusion of those who are different and outside the group, or when such people are seen as inferior. Children who participate in at least one extra curricular activity have a more positive view of their peers and their community. Membership of groups that engage in charitable acts or community service boosts social trust too.

This would be the time to invent a Strengths Builder like *Save the World*, to consult with the children about ways they can help this community and the wider community and to let them practice their teamwork (and leadership) skills in the service of others. Such activities can be as simple as litter picking or as elaborate and wide ranging as you wish.

Within school, a focus on *co-operative groups*, groups of children who do not usually work together and who can bring their separate strengths to a group task would also be helpful. In a surprisingly large number of classes there are children who literally never work together - how does that help the class as a whole to consider itself a team?

Strengths spotting is a good activity for such groups to start with and a class strengths spotting exercise, where you make a poster of ALL your class strengths can direct children's attention to their peers in positive ways. As with leadership, *Speakers and Listeners* and *Brilliant Listening* are important Strengths Builders for building social skills.

Stories that show teamwork in action might include *The Musicians of Bremen*, which I retell as *The Four Musicians,* and a Chinese Tale, *The Magic Paintbrush*. You will find others as you look out for them.

Honesty, Integrity and Authenticity

Integrity is perhaps one of the hardest strengths to explain to children. They grasp honesty easily enough, but integrity and authenticity go beyond this to being a person who is open and straightforward and who acts in accordance with their values. A person with integrity and authenticity practices what they preach and treats others gently and with care, being sensitive to their needs.

Authentic people are well liked and make successful managers and good friends. They tend to be happy, empathic and successful in life. There is a suggestion that overly controlling environments may lead to inauthentic behaviour, so those in authority need to encourage choice if they wish integrity and authenticity to develop. *Story Telling* always allows choice. You, the story teller, are in charge of words and tone and the word pictures you create. *Create a Story Space* and other, similarly open ended activities allow small choices within our somewhat over prescribed curriculum. *Philosophy*, which gives pupils the opportunity for self expression and for exploring their own values will also support the development of integrity. Lying and inauthentic behaviour may develop as self defence against controlling or abusive environments.

Self awareness is an important element of honesty and integrity – if we are not honest with ourselves how can we be honest with others?

The Strengths Builders that encourage *Reflection* will all help self awareness, as will the meditations. There is a particularly lovely moving meditation I have used at this time of year as it links with the abundance of green in nature. It is a *Tree Meditation* and is based on a series of Tai Chi moves I learned from story teller Lynn Barbour. Starting with hands in a triangle in front of the solar plexis while quiet music plays, the children are asked to take three deep, slow but very quiet breaths. Then the tree grows and their hands open in front of their chests. Once more they are asked to take three deep, slow, quiet breaths. Then the tree grows some more and their hands lift and form branches as they take three more breaths. Then, imagining the sap as green, peaceful light rising within them, the children can send out that peaceful light to fill the school and one another. Lastly, autumn leaves flutter down and their hands fall to rest lightly on their knees. I have done this in assembly with children as young as 4 and it works beautifully to calm them and give them a tiny space in a busy day to be still – without stillness, it is hard to know ourselves.

Children can be encouraged to become more honest. Interestingly, less specific instructions, for example, 'Be honest,' are more effective than specific ones, 'Do this,' 'Don't do that' – most probably because more general instructions invite children to think and decide for themselves A community where honesty is valued highly will encourage children to value this important strength in themselves and others.

The Sword in the Stone

When these islands were young, hundreds of years ago, King Uther Pendragon died. Though he had once had a son, the boy had been taken away as a baby and now no-one knew who he was or where he lived.

And so there was no son to follow King Uther as king. Without a king, every knight tried to gain power for himself and laws were broken and the ordinary people were mistreated by the rich and powerful. And when things were at their worst Merlin the magician went to London, to the palace of the Archbishop of Canterbury, and told the Archbishop to call the rich and powerful together in the church on Christmas Day to pray for a miracle.

And the Archbishop did as Merlin said. When the lords and the nobles left the church, there in the churchyard was a great stone, and in the stone was a sword, and above it the words, 'Whoever pulls this sword from this stone is the true born king of all England.' Then the lords rushed forward and tried to pull the sword from the stone. They pulled and pulled and pulled – but none could make it move so much as an inch.

'The true king of England is not here,' said Merlin. 'Summon all the knights in the land to a tournament on New Year's Day so that each one may try to pull the sword from the stone.

So from every corner of England knights travelled to London. And among them went Sir Ector, a brave and noble knight with his son, Sir Kay and his foster son, Arthur. On the morning of the tournament Sir Kay was so excited, for it was his first tournament since he had been made knight, that he forgot his sword and sent Arthur back to the house to fetch it. But when he got to the house, Arthur found the door locked and the people in it nowhere to be seen.

Arthur was angry – he loved his foster brother, Kay, and was determined to find him a sword. Then Arthur remembered seeing a sword in a churchyard, stuck in a stone, so he ran straight there, pulled out the sword easily and took it to Sir Kay. Sir Kay knew that it was not his sword. He knew it was the sword from the stone, so he took it to his father and said, 'Look, father, I am the true king of England.'

Sir Ector said not a word but took both boys back to the church-yard. Then, taking a bible, he made Sir Kay put his hand upon it and asked him, 'Where did you get this sword?' Sir Kay was at heart an honest boy and so he answered, 'Arthur brought it to me.' Then Sir Ector asked Arthur, 'Where did you get this sword?' And Arthur said, 'I pulled it out of that stone over there.'

Sir Ector put the sword back into the stone. He tried to pull it out. He pulled and pulled and pulled – but he could not make it move so much as an inch. Then Sir Kay tried. He pulled and pulled and pulled – but he could not make it move so much as an inch. Then Arthur tried. And the sword slid smoothly and easily out of the stone. And Sir Ector and Sir Kay knelt to Arthur and called him king.

But the other nobles were furious. 'Will we accept this boy as king?' they cried. And they demanded that the sword be put back into the stone so that all the knights could try again on the feast of 12th Night, 12 days after Christmas.

So that is what happened but though all the knights pulled and pulled and pulled – none could make it move so much as an inch. Only Arthur could pull the sword out of the stone. But still the knights and nobles were not satisfied. They demanded that the sword be replaced in the stone so that all the knights could try again on the feast of Candlemas, the 2nd of February.

So that is what happened but though all the knights pulled and pulled and pulled – none could make it move so much as an inch. Only Arthur could pull the sword out of the stone. But STILL the knights and nobles were not satisfied. They demanded that the sword be replaced in the stone so that all the knights could try again on the feast of Easter.

So that is what happened but though all the knights pulled and pulled and pulled – none could make it move so much as an inch. Again, only Arthur could pull the sword out of the stone But STILL the knights and nobles were not satisfied.

But then, on the feast of Pentecost, seven weeks after Easter, when Arthur had pulled the sword out of the stone yet again, and the knights and nobles were STILL not satisfied, the ordinary people, people like you and me, who wanted a king to bring order and peace to England, began to cheer for Arthur and to call him King, and at last the knights and nobles gave in and they too, knelt to Arthur, the true king of all England.

And Arthur knelt and put his sword upon the altar. Then the crown was placed upon his head and Arthur swore to serve the people of England as their true king all the days of his life.

FIFTEEN

Endings

ENDINGS ARE IMPORTANT – and painful and often avoided! Teachers, I suspect, are not good at endings simply because they care so much about the children they teach and saying goodbye to people we care about is always difficult.

The end of a school day is important – is it positive and hopeful, or bad tempered and rushed? The end of a lesson is as important as the beginning – does it bring a sense of completion, of work well done? Is there time for reflection on the work, on how the lesson progressed, on what was learned and how well strengths were used?

The end of the school year is even more important. A good end to the school year is perhaps the single most important preparation for the following year. If we end this year well, we lay the foundations for a good start in September. However, endings are difficult things. Endings mean saying goodbye, they entail a sense of sadness and loss. These are uncomfortable emotions that most of us prefer to avoid. Endings, even little ones, echo bigger endings in our lives, reminding us at an unconscious level of previous endings and of future endings. Endings are like a little death – they remind us that all things must cease, including ourselves.

Sometimes previous experiences make endings particularly painful. I attended a year long course on group dynamics. Towards the end of the course one group member, a psychologist, expressed her dread of endings. She explained that as a child she had had to move school frequently because of her father's work and she hated saying goodbye. On the last day of the course she was absent – the emotions around endings were simply too much for her to bear.

For the children we teach, endings may contain very ambivalent feelings too, a mixture of excitement and relief, anxiety, sadness and even anger. Anything where emotions are very mixed is hard work for adults, let alone children, to understand and manage well. Children may feel holidays as an experience of being abandoned by a loved and trusted teacher and feel both sadness and anger as a result. If home is less than happy, this feeling may be particularly acute and result in poor behaviour towards the end of term. Teachers say, 'They're tired' or 'They're excited' and they may be. But they may also be trying to express this anger that they don't really understand. Or they may be trying to prove to themselves, by provoking you, that you are 'horrid' so they won't really miss you, and that school is 'rubbish' so that they'll be better off without it. Poor behaviour at the end of term – and you may see it before each holiday including half terms - is actually a compliment. It is a child's way of saying, without having to say it, how much you really mean to them.

Thinking about endings, by having an 'Endings' festival, is one way of beginning to manage the complex emotions that are involved and for helping children to do the same. The Endings festival need not last for the full final half term – it might last a month or just two or three weeks. By spending time thinking about ending, about saying goodbye, you take some of the sting out of the final day – like letting steam out of a pressure cooker bit by bit rather than all at once. The Endings festival has a focus on reflection, on looking back and remembering what was good, what was enjoyable and on thinking about how to take those good memories away with us.

There should be time for children to reflect on what they have achieved, on what has gone well for them. There should also be time for adults to do this. Make time to sit and look back on what you, as a teacher, have achieved this year. What has gone well, what particular happy memories will you take away with you? A staff meeting devoted to sharing and celebrating the achievements of individual staff and of the school as a whole would be appropriate. In recent years there has been too much focus on what schools need to do to improve, and insufficient acknowledgement of what they are already doing well. Head Teachers might hold a special meal for staff and encourage them to share successes and progress over the last year, together with their hopes for the future over the next year and beyond.

For children for whom this is a final year in school, I suggest acknowledging this fact right from September. It is their final year here, and that is both sad and exciting. They know it is their last year, and saying so occasionally, putting into words all that this implies, lets children come to terms with needing to move on and let go of this stage of life and allows them to do so positively.

Humans eat to avoid uncomfortable emotions and to comfort themselves. That is why parties and food on a last day are so common. The notion of 'comfort food' is now highly disapproved of in our health obsessed age. But feasting together to say goodbye is an ancient human custom and there is no reason why modern anxieties should be allowed to drive out ancient wisdom – we all need comfort food sometimes. Food, preparing it and eating it together, should be part of the Ending festival as it should be part of every other festival. We can worry about 'healthy eating' when it is appropriate to do so – not at a feast!

Having said that, the strengths I have linked with this festival are strengths of temperance or self restraint, strengths that protect us from excess, forgiveness, self control and prudence. Forgiveness seems an apt strength to link with saying goodbye, a letting go of hurt and resentment and a deliberate choice to remember instead what was good. Self control helps us to manage the difficult emotions around endings and to choose to act and think in appropriate and constructive ways. Prudence is a wonderful word – so old fashioned but so important! Prudence is about making good choices for the future and though it may seem a little boring and unexciting and is certainly unfashionable, the fact remains that people who make prudent choices are healthier, happier and richer than those who don't!

The stories that are told during the endings festival can echo these themes. At the end of the chapter I include an Orkney story, that of *The Selkie Wife*. It is a story of a goodbye. I like to use other sea legends too, because for me, the sea is an excellent metaphor for change and moving on. There are lots of sea legends to choose from, tails of mer people and selkies, seals who change into human form for a time. Traditional stories are often about prudence – they are one of the main vehicles adults have always used to urge children to be careful – don't talk to strangers, don't build your house of bricks, don't eat dodgy looking gingerbread cottages!

What can be lovely (and one school I have worked with does this) is to make deliberate parallels between the very first day, in September, and the very last day in July. The assemblies echo one another and the children receive a brand new book on the first day and are read it again on the last day. Such echoes feel profoundly satisfying and contribute to a calm and positive day for staff and children alike.

Endings assemblies are a particularly important part of this festival. You might take the Strengths Builder *Pearls* and hold a school pearls assembly, where each class shares its happiest event. Teachers could share their pearls from the year and the Head Teacher could reflect back on his or her own pearl. If you have had photo albums to collect happy memories in, some of the best photos could be shared and explained.

One idea for a simple ritual for leavers is to prepare a single, large magic memory pearl, full of their happiest memories from the year, not to take away with them but to leave behind, for the school to treasure and remember them by. They might put this 'magic memory pearl' in a pool of water, a water feature or a symbolic 'sea' created in the middle of the hall from blue cloth. Building the 'sea' might form part of the assembly.

Forgiveness

Forgiveness is an important strength for building good relationships. A tendency to brood on wrongs and to harbour resentment can only undermine our relationships with those with whom we live and work. Conversely, letting go of grudges, thinking the best of people rather than the worse, will benefit not only our relationships but also our own health and well-being. Harbouring resentment hurts mostly us ourselves.

Forgiveness is valued in all religious traditions but it is not a specifically religious strength. The Forgiveness Project collects stories of extraordinary forgiveness from around the world that are inspiring and humbling to read. These are stories of forgiveness on a large scale, which most of us will not be called on to emulate.

However, in the day to day bustle of school life there will be ample opportunities for letting go of niggles and grudges that we can use to build our own and our pupils' capacity to forgive.

Forgiveness seems to be a factor of age – adults are more forgiving than children and older adults are more forgiving than younger ones. For this reason, modelling becomes the most crucial factor for encouraging the development of this important strength. We need to demonstrate that we value forgiveness and regard it as an act of courage, both by our own actions and by the stories that we tell.

Forgiveness involves three things – our *feelings* towards somebody who has hurt us, our *thoughts* about the person who has hurt us, and our *behaviour* towards a person who has hurt us. These three aspects can be addressed through using different Strengths Builders.

Forgiveness is closely related to empathy, the ability to understand the feelings of others. *Good Bits / Bad Bits* is a Strengths Builder that encourages empathy and so is *How Do I Feel?* We have to be able to notice and understand our own feelings before we can understand those of other people. *WOW* is a Strengths Builder we can use to directly challenge our resentful feelings. It is one of the Strengths Builders used for tolerance and can be repeated to encourage forgiveness, too. It is a conscious effort to feel more positively towards somebody who is annoying us or who has hurt us in some way. You might use *Wishing Others Well* as a visualisation game, encouraging children to picture themselves giving a good gift to someone they like and then to someone they don't like, saying something kind to someone they find easy to get on with and to someone they don't find easy to get on with. This will send the important message that we can choose to work on our feelings towards others and that you value forgiveness yourself.

The ability to see another's point of view is also an important aspect of forgiveness that we can encourage through Strengths Builders like *Philosophy* and *Opinion Line*.

Learning to control our thoughts is another important aspect of forgiveness. The tendency to brood undermines forgiveness and leads to depression as well as poor relationships. *Eeyore Thinking* challenges this rumination so it would be appropriate to use as a Strengths Builder for forgiveness. So does meditation (meditation is all about learning to control our thoughts), so any of the meditations your class enjoys can be forgiveness Strengths Builders.

The final aspect of forgiveness, how we act towards those who have wronged us, can also be addressed through *WOW* – you might send WOW cards to people you don't necessarily get on with. Also, any of the Strengths Builders for kindness would be useful here because true kindness is not restricted to being nice to our friends.

Stories that echo the themes of forgiveness, besides very explicit true life stories such as those from the Forgiveness Project, might be drawn from faith traditions or from traditional tales. *The Selkie Wife* is a favourite of mine. I also like the story of St Columba, who brought the Christian faith to Scotland as an act of repentance. He stole a valuable book and caused a war – very saintly! But in the end he found forgiveness and learned to let go himself.

Self control

There are two elements to self control – refraining from doing things on impulse or in response to stimuli, and doing things that lead us to accomplish our goals and to meet the standards we set for ourselves or that others set for us. It is failures of self control that lead to many of society's problems – alcoholism, drug abuse, violence, debt, obesity and anti social behaviour. Children who are high in self control do better in school, have better self esteem, fewer problems with anger and better relationships.

There are indications that self control can be developed and that, like a muscle, it can be built with practice. It is also important to note that self control is tiring – if we exercise it a lot in the morning there will be less energy to exert it in the afternoon. Practically this means that children with difficulties in this area, with high levels of anger or anxiety for example, will need a chance to rest after an activity that requires a lot of self control from them. Building balance and 'down time' into the curriculum is therefore important, and teachers need to be aware of which situations tax a child's self control the most so that they can space these out if possible.

Self awareness is an important aspect of self control – we need to be aware of what the self is feeling and thinking if we are to exert control over it. Strengths Builders that encourage self awareness will be important here – activities like *LAUGHS* and a *Feelings Story Scroll*, for example, where you tell a story and invite children to identify and then draw or doodle the feelings in it and the scenes that show these feelings. Again, *How Do I Feel?* encourages self awareness. *Meditation* is considered an excellent way to build self control so this, too, can be used frequently and as an individual Strengths Builder for children who really need more of this strength. *Create a Story Space* is a lovely way to build self control and one that is also quite calming and restful.

When actions are habitual we need less self control to make us carry them out – that is partly why Celebrating Strengths aims to build positive habits of thought, speech and behaviour. That leaves our self control free for less common occurrences. Forming positive habits and letting good structure and routine govern much of life means that we can save our reserves of self control for when it matters.

We can also exercise our self control like a muscle. Making a habit of little acts of self control like politeness, good posture, smart dress can build self discipline and help people to exercise greater self control in times of stress – little changes make a difference and add up to greater change.

Change the Future is another Strengths Builder that uses the fact that we can rehearse certain behaviours in our minds so that, when the time comes, they feel more automatic, more habitual. You might do *Change the Future* with an individual child with a specific area where they find self control difficult, or with a whole class that is facing a challenge. You encourage the children to relax, you might play soothing music, and then you lead them in an imaginative story, where they picture the future challenging event and imagine themselves behaving just as they would wish to behave. Do this a few times and the desired behaviour will become easier, more automatic. Athletes do this because it has been shown to be effective.

It is also helpful to self control to have explicit goals to aim for and to see how we are doing – if we lose track of our progress we are more likely to go off the rails. Using *Where There's a Will* and making maps so children can chart their progress – putting those charts up in a prominent place to remind them of their goals – will all be helpful strategies. Other Strengths Builders that encourage optimism can also be used again here, *WWW* or *Eeyore Thoughts*.

Savouring is a good activity for the end of term. Partly because it is a meditation that encourages self control, partly because one cause of over eating is our failure to savour our food in the first place, and partly because there are uncomfortable emotions flying about at this time of year, which render us more likely to eat for comfort. Recognising this, *Savouring* can be used as a counter measure.

There are plenty of traditional stories that highlight the bad end that results from a lack of self control. One of these is *Rumpelstiltskin* – the miller failed to exercise appropriate self control and boasted about his daughter once too often. There are lots of different versions of *Rumpelstiltskin* as I noted above – you might collect and tell some of these.

Prudence

Prudence is a wonderful strength – the more I work with it the more fond of it I become. It is old fashioned, hard working, unexciting, over looked, the Cinderella of the strengths list, but utterly essential if we are to live fulfilling and happy lives! Let's hear it for prudence! Prudence is, apart from being an amazing old Quaker name, about making good choices. Choosing to eat sensibly, choosing not to over indulge in alcohol (or not too often, at any rate), choosing to spend our money wisely and to save where we can, choosing to exercise and to balance our work and our leisure – work-life balance is after all an aspect of prudence.

Prudence now has rather narrow and largely economic connotations, but going back to writers and thinkers as early as Aristotle, it had a much broader and more positive meaning. Prudence, according to Aristotle, is a form of practical wisdom. The prudent individual is neither reckless nor rigid, neither impulsive nor compulsive, but balanced and flexible. A prudent person is one who considers what life is for and how this may be best achieved, one who balances short term pleasures against long term goals. They are forward thinking and conscientious, not miserly or narrow.

Prudence is important in the exercise of other strengths – sometimes it is prudent not to persist, hope must be balanced by realism, curiosity needs occasionally to be curbed and so on.

It is this broader, positive notion of prudence that I wish to encourage in schools. Children with this kind of practical wisdom tend to be happier and to do well in schools while adults who exhibit it are not only healthier and happier but also enjoy more job satisfaction and are generally fun to know.

Prudence implies the ability to reflect, to adopt a thoughtful rather than thoughtless approach to life. Strengths Builders that encourage reflection, like *Pearls* and *WWW* and *Reflections* itself will all help to achieve this. Prudence also requires imagination, the ability to imagine a future for oneself in which a goal has been achieved. Any Strengths Builders that encourage imagination are therefore relevant, so *Story Telling* and *Create a Story Space* could also be used.

While little work has been done on how to build prudence it seems reasonable to assume that chaotic lives that lack structure or any forward planning may undermine its growth, as well as a lack of autonomy - the sense that there is no point in having good goals because there is nothing that one can do to achieve them. The structure, routine and predictability of school, which Celebrating Strengths is designed to enhance, will help to build a sense that the future is predictable and is therefore worth thinking about, as will Strengths Builders like *Where There's a Will*.

Another aspect of prudence is the ability to make and stick to personal rules and overcome impulsiveness. Letting children consider and make personal rules will support this aspect of prudence. You might call it *'I'm in charge of me'* and ask children to make a rule that will help them to achieve a positive goal – something like 'I will always read my work before I hand it in' and, since they are in charge, they can reward themselves when they stick to their rule.

There are plenty of stories that reflect this strength – most fairy tales in fact. Making good choices, thinking ahead, are all traits we instinctively know are good for children and which generations of adults have striven to inculcate via stories like *Little Red Riding Hood* and *Rumpelstiltskin*.

The Selkie Wife

Selkies dancing on the shore
Dancing as they did before
Dancing on for hours and hours
See the selkie dancers.

Long ago on the islands of Orkney, far to the north of here, there lived a lonely fisherman. At the end of his day's work this fisherman would walk along the beach below his hut, enjoying the peace of the evening and the beauty of the shining sea. But the fisherman lived alone and longed for someone with whom he could share that peace and that beauty.

One evening, as the fisherman was walking along the beach, he heard voices, calling and laughing. The fisherman walked further along the beach and he saw people dancing. The fisherman walked still further and, behind a rock, he found seal skins, soft, silky seal skins, and the fisherman realised that these were not real people, they were selkies or seals who had taken human form so that they could dance upon the sand just for that one night in the whole year.

The fisherman was so lonely that he stayed behind the rock to watch them dance all night long. And he watched one selkie woman, the most beautiful selkie woman of all, more than all the others and as he watched her he fell in love.

At dawn, when the sun came up, the seal people ran down the sand, pulled on their seal skins and dived back into the shining sea. All except one, the most beautiful seal woman of all, who couldn't find her seal skin. She could not find it because the fisherman had hidden it in his pocket.

The seal woman ran to the fisherman and told him she had lost her seal skin and begged him to help her find it. The fisherman told the seal woman that he had lost his heart to her and begged her to stay with him and to be his wife.

The seal woman looked at the fisherman and there was love shining in her deep, dark seal eyes and she said, yes, she would marry him. But, she said, she could only stay with him for seven years. At the end of that time, she said, she would have to return to the sea, where she belonged, or she would surely die.

The fisherman agreed and the two of them were married the very next day.After that the fisherman and his seal wife walked together along the beach, enjoying the peace of the evening and the beauty of the shining sea. And soon they had children to walk with them too and the fisherman's happiness was complete.

But seven years passed all too quickly and the seal wife began to miss the sea. Her skin became dry and her deep, dark eyes became cloudy. Her hands and her feet hurt her and she began to find it harder to go for walks along the beach.

At last, one day, she went to the fisherman and asked him to give her back her seal skin. The fisherman looked at his wife and he could not bear the thought of saying goodbye to her and he said, no.

After that, the seal woman stayed at home more and more, leaving her family to walk along the beach without her. One day, when she was alone in the house, the selkie wife was cleaning when, hidden in an old jug, she found a key. It was the key to a wooden chest that the fisherman always kept locked. The selkie wife took the key and unlocked the chest. She opened the lid and there, inside, was her seal skin.

The fisherman and his children were walking together along the beach enjoying the peace of the evening and the beauty of the shining sea. But, suddenly, their hearts filled, not with happiness, but with fear - for there was their mother running down the sand towards them. And she was wearing her seal skin.

She dived into the water and disappeared and they thought that they would never see her again. But then her head rose above the waves and she looked at her children and told them that she loved them and would always remember them.

Then she dived into the water and disappeared and they thought that they would never see her again. But once more her head rose above the waves, and she looked at her husband with love shining in her deep, dark seal eyes. She told him she loved him and would always remember him, but she had to go back to the sea where she belonged or else she would surely die.

Then she dived into the waves and swam away.

The family did not see her again that night. But sometimes, as they walked along the beach in the evenings, enjoying the peace and the beauty of the shining sea, they would see a seal head rise up out of the waves and they would see love shining in its deep, dark seal eyes. And it is said, though I don't know if it is true, that after this the fisherman caught more fish than any other man on Orkney because a certain seal was helping him.

Selkies dancing on the shore
Dancing as they did before
Dancing on for hours and hours
See the selkie dancers.

SIXTEEN

Creating Your Own Festivals

THE FESTIVALS I have described were designed for one school and then developed further in others. You might want to design one or more festivals for your own school, to celebrate its unique strengths. What do you need to do to create your own festival?

Starting Point

A starting point might be a local tradition or existing festival, a festival from your own faith or another faith, or a school tradition – either an existing one or one you wish to establish. You could start with a season if you wished, and have an autumn or spring festival, or a summer festival. You might decide to start with elements and to think about air, water, fire and earth at different times of the year. You might start with an activity you already enjoy or would like to start enjoying – dancing or singing or flying kites, or cooking. You will already have school traditions that might fit well into a festival or even form the starting point of one.

It would be entirely appropriate for a school with a large Muslim population, for example, to add an important faith festival to their own cycle. You might still keep Advent and Easter, for example, because they tell the central stories of Christianity and it is important for all children in our country to understand and know these stories. However, you could add Muslim faith stories alongside them. Alternatively, you could change the festivals entirely, call them something different and include the elements which Muslims know to be appropriate and essential.

People from the Muslim faith will know the stories, the foods, the songs, the games that might be played. You will also see the links that can be most appropriately made to the strengths and virtues, which are universal.

It would also be entirely appropriate for a school that was predominantly Christian, for example, to decide to celebrate a Jewish or Islamic festival precisely because its pupils did not usually meet children of other faiths. If you decided to do this, I would suggest inviting a member of that faith to come and help you to design appropriate celebrations and then to come and share them with you. Building bridges between faiths is essential and this would be one good way of working towards that goal.

What Are the Ingredients of Each Festival?

- *Strengths*

A link with strengths is essential but you can link whatever strengths seem appropriate to you. My links feel appropriate to me but you might feel other strengths could be highlighted at particular festivals – there is no right or wrong here. The principle that all strengths are focussed on yearly is important, since we get more of what we focus on and we would not wish to miss out an essential strength or one that is a top strength for some community members. However, *when* we focus on them is not set in stone. Make links that seem appropriate, visit some more than once – adapt and be creative.

- *Reflection*

Time to be still and think is an essential aspect of all the festivals. Pick at least one reflective Strengths Builder, either *Pearls,* or a *Meditation,* or *Reflections* itself and incorporate it either into the class work or into an assembly or both. True education requires 'down time,' time for recollection and reflection. There is not enough of it in schools - either for adults or children. Build some in and guard it, vigorously!

- *Stories*

When you have decided on the strengths to link to a new festival, think of stories that echo those strengths and show them in action. They can be faith stories – some of them probably should be – and secular stories, traditional or folk tales.

Do find local stories from your area. *The Lore of the Land* would help you do this. It is so important that children hear stories from their place and get a feel for local traditions. The internet is a great place for finding stories but you will need to adapt them and make them tell-able. Simplify, change words and style to suit you, play with the story until it feels right. If you are anything like me it will still change every time you tell it! Alternatively, you can email me at **jenny@cappeu.org** and say, 'We need a story about x' – I like a challenge!

You can also include personal, community stories. At my daughter's school, they have established a prize giving tradition at the end of year 11 and year 13. I was moved to hear the story of one of the prizes, awarded by the parents of a former pupil who died young and tragically. It is given to a student who has overcome adversity and shown great courage. The worthy recipient in my daughter's year received a standing ovation from his peers. There was not a dry eye in the house! Every time this great prize is given, the story of the teenager whose life was cut short will be retold. She will, rightly, be remembered by her community in a positive and life affirming way.

- *Celebration*

Be creative here! Compose songs, make up dances, read, write and perform poems and plays, have parties, go on picnics, go on long walks, hold competitions. There are as many ways to celebrate as there are human beings.

- *Food*

This is a must. Celebrations involve feasting (please turn aside, healthy eating co-ordinators). There is a time for self restraint and self control and, as I have said before, this time is **not** at a feast. Preparing and sharing food together is a basic human need and it is at the heart of building strong communities. The children should come to associate *this* festival with *this* particular delicious food. If it is a summer festival, that food can be fruit by all means, but *not* because the government tells us to, but because we want to, please. Sometimes, we need to put first the needs of the community to feast together. Prepare delicious food, and if it involves chocolate or biscuits, it involves chocolate or biscuits!

- *Smell*

Smells are important memory boosters. Link the strengths to certain smells and whenever children smell those smells they will remember those strengths – it is sneaky teaching par excellence.

Smells bring back emotional memories too, because the parts of our brain associated with smell, and with memory and emotion are closely linked. The pleasures, excitement and specialness of your festivals will come back to children very strongly if you associate them with certain smells. You might always cook certain foods or always bring a particular plant or flower into school. Those will be the main scents to work with. You may think of others.

- *Colour*

I associated the traditional Christian colour of fasting, purple, with Advent and Easter and fairly arbitrary colours for the other festivals. Think of a colour that compliments your festival and let the school environment echo the colour throughout the festival.

- *Music*

Choose appropriate music for your festival, depending on what mood you wish to foster. We have used Allegri's *Misereri* for Advent and Easter, for example, and a lovely peaceful tape called *Zen and the*

Art of Relaxation for Our Community. You might want something up beat and tango-like, or a folk melody. If you keep *this* music for *this* festival, again you are teaching indirectly and building associations between the music, and the ideas and strengths of the festival – more sneaky teaching, like the colours, above.

• *Individual, Classroom, Whole School*

Give some thought to the different levels at which the festival is celebrated and experienced. Individual adults and children can use the strengths of the festival as much as they can at home and at school. One school sends leaflets home to parents telling them what strengths they are focussing on at school, telling them a little about each strength, and how they might follow up the work with their children and spot those strengths at home.

Individuals whose top strengths are the focus for attention will particularly enjoy extra opportunities for using them and for taking a lead in showing others how to use them. You can make small cards with Strengths Builders on them which can be used by individuals in odd moments, as rewards or as incentives.

In class, use existing Strengths Builders or adapt them or invent new ones – the children will enjoy thinking of ideas.

At the whole school level you will already be thinking of whole school events, assemblies and celebrations. Make sure *everyone* in the community knows they are invited to share with you – caretakers and cooks, kitchen staff and governors. They are all part of your community and the more often everyone gathers together the stronger the community will be.

- *Enjoyment*

This is fundamental – if it is stressful or miserable it is not enhancing learning or community.

Festivals are enduring. Create a tradition and link some strengths to it, and you will have created something that outlasts your own involvement with both the children and the school. You will have created happy memories and an enduring, positive tradition. You will have made a small change that leaves the world a better place. However, though festivals feel the same each year, they're not. They do actually change, little by little, and evolve, as we do. Sometimes they may even need to give way to completely new ones. Trust your instincts and judgement, and go with the flow.

SEVENTEEN

In Conclusion: Where to Begin?

WHERE DO YOU start if you wish to Celebrate Strengths in your school? Anywhere at all, with anything. Start with any of the threads, the strengths, the stories or the festivals. Start at any level, with a special assembly (whole school level), a Strengths Builder or story (classroom level), an individual Strengths Builder or assessment of the strengths (individual level).

You need only do one thing to make a difference, because small changes add up. We change the world by tiny individual acts of honesty, courage, kindness and integrity, by celebrating our own strengths and those of other people, by using our strengths, just a little more, each day and helping others to do the same.

You don't have to change the whole world, just the little part of it you meet day by day, one strength at a time, one story at a time, one child at a time.

So celebrate strengths, your own, those of your school and those of your pupils. Using your strengths a little more is the smallest thing you can do to make the biggest difference. And I hope - because hope is one of MY top strengths - that this book supports and helps you to do just that and to make a positive difference in your own life, in the life of your school, in the lives of your students.

Chapter 1: Introduction

10   "I have based the strengths in Celebrating Strengths on the work of two psychologists, Chris Peterson and Martin Seligman..."

The list of strengths used in Celebrating Strengths builds on Peterson and Seligman's VIA Classification of strengths. The background information on the strengths is taken from Peterson, C. & Seligman, M. E. P. (2004).
Character Strengths and Virtues: A Handbook and Classification. Oxford: Oxford University Press

10   "Teachers can test their own strengths online..."

You can test your own VIA strengths test at **www.authentichappiness.org** and **www.viastrengths.org** and also find there a children's VIA suitable for children of 10 and over.

12   "I have written a whole book just on this subject alone..."

Fox Eades, J. M. (2006). *Classroom Tales*. London: Jessica Kingsley.

13   "I belong to an international organisation called the Positive Workplace Alliance"

The Positive Workplace Alliance provides teleconference discussion groups for people who wish to develop the use of positive psychology in the workplace. For more information contact: **jocelyn@positiveworkplace.com**, or **amanda@positiveworkplace.com**

Chapter 2: Positive Psychology in Education

19   "Studies now show that doing exactly that can have a significant effect on reducing depression and increasing happiness."

See, for example, Seligman, M. E. P., Steen, T. A., Park, N., & Peterson, C. (2005). Positive Psychology Progress, Empirical Validation of Interventions. *American Psychologist, 60* (5), 410-421. (available free at **http://www.authentichappiness.sas.upenn.edu/images/apaarticle.pdf**)

20   "…with Fredrickson's 'broaden-and-build' theory of positive emotions…"

See Fredrickson, B. (1998). What Good Are Positive Emotions? *Review of General Psychology, 2* (3), 300-319.

22   "A study into the low achievement of children in inner cities in America…"

Ben-Shahar, T. (2006). Positive Psychology Lecture 2, *'Why Positive Psychology?'* 7/2/06
Tal gave a series of lectures on positive psychology at Harvard in 2006. They were the best attended in the history of Harvard. You can watch them, free, on the internet at **http://isites.harvard.edu/icb/icb.do?keyword=k14790&pageid=icb.page69189**

23   "Positive emotions produce cognitive changes."

Fredrickson (ibid), page 308

23   "There are three areas that Seligman highlights…"

Seligman, M. E. P. (2002). *Authentic Happiness.* London: Nicholas Brealey Publishing

25   "The second and third groups did better on the test."

See Seligman (ibid), page 36.

25   "Psychologists call this kind of story telling 'explanatory style'."

For more information on explanatory style in children, see Seligman, M. E. P. (1995). *The Optimistic Child.* New York: HarperPerennial.

28   "The psychologist Chris Peterson argues that flow is rarely experienced by pupils during any school activity…"

Peterson, C. (2006). *A Primer in Positive Psychology.* Oxford: Oxford University Press

29   "I am indebted to the psychologist Tal Ben-Shahar for the concept of 'stretch-zones.'"

Ben-Shahar, T. (2006). Positive Psychology Lecture 11, 9/3/06

32   "Seligman argues that optimistic thinking is a skill that can be learned…"

Seligman, M. E. P. (1995). *The Optimistic Child.* New York: HarperPerennial.

32   "These are skills that can be taught and improved."

A book that explains more about the concept of resilience is Reivich, K.,
& Shatte, A. (2002). *The Resilience Factor*. New York: Broadway Books.

Chapter 3: Strengths and Strengths Gym

39   "A recent study of US newly qualified teachers showed that..."

Information on teacher's strengths came from Peterson, C. Lecture 2 in
Positive Psychology and Coaching 28/9/06 given by MentorCoach

Chapter 4: Stories and Story Telling

49   "*Goodbye Mog* is a book about death."

Kerr, J. (2002). *Goodbye Mog*. London: HarperCollins.

49   "I had written an entire book on stories and story telling..."

Fox Eades, J. M. (2006). *Classroom Tales*. London: Jessica Kingsley.

58   "The fact that *What a Mess* made Mrs Eades giggle out loud..."

Muir, F. (1982). *Super What-a-Mess*. London: Picture Corgi.

59   "The twentieth century psychologist Bettelheim used this aspect of
hopefulness..."

Bettelheim, B. (1976). *The Uses of Enchantment*. London: Penguin Books.

61   "...that was influenced by a Montessori RE method called Godly Play.

For more information on Godly Play see Berryman, J. (1995) *Teaching
Godly Play; The Sunday Morning Handbook* Nashville: Abingdon Press

Chapter 5: Festivals and Celebrations

65   "...unique book called The Emotional Experience of Learning and
Teaching."

Salzberger-Wittenberg, I., Williams, G., & Osborne, E. (1983). *The
Emotional Experience of Learning and Teaching*. London: Karnac.

76   "Studies have shown that choral singing increases immunity..."

Sieghart, M. (2007) *Why take Prozac when you can sing Prokofiev?* In *The
Times*, January 18, 2007.

80   "Can you think of any additional ideas to expand your cycle of cele-
      brations?"

      The website **www.gratefulness.org** has a calendar of secular and faith
      celebrations from around the world. It is a wonderful site to explore
      and use as part of your festivals and celebrations.

Chapter 6: Celebrating Strengths in the Individual

87   "Alex Linley writes about listening for strengths..."

      Linley, P. A. (2006). *Listening and Observing for Strengths*. CAPP
      Pathfinder Paper #3. Coventry, UK: Centre for Applied Positive
      Psychology.

93   "Children learn their explanatory style..."

      For more information on explanatory style see Seligman, M. E. P. (1995)
      The Optimistic Child. New York: HarperPerennial.

Chapter 7: Celebrating Strengths in the Classroom

104   "I include different kinds of meditation..."

      For learning to meditate yourself, I highly recommend Wilson, P.
      (2007). *The Quiet*. London: Macmillan. He strips away the jargon and
      makes meditation accessible to everyone.

105   "This is a technique taught by a Buddhist writer called Pema
      Chodron."

      Chodron, P. (2001). *The Wisdom of No Escape*. London: HarperCollins.

109   "Philosophy with children is an excellent positive tool..."

      I would recommend Haynes, J. (2002). *Children as Philosophers*. London:
      Routledge. Or you could contact the charity, Sapere,
      http://www.sapere.net, to find out more about philosophy with chil-
      dren.

Chapter 8: Celebrating Strengths in the Wider School

115   "In a Harvard lecture on positive psychology..."

      Ben-Shahar, T. (2006). Positive Psychology Lecture 5, '*Beliefs as self
      fulfilling prophecies*' 16/2/2006.

Tal Ben-Shahar is a psychologist, writer and great teacher. I would thoroughly recommend his book, *The Question of Happiness*, (2002), London: Writers Club Press. Short but profound.

Tal gave a series of lectures on positive psychology at Harvard in 2006. They were the best attended in the history of Harvard. You can watch them, free, on the internet at:
http://isites.harvard.edu/icb/icb.do?keyword=k14790&pageid=icb.pag e69189

Chapter 9: Beginnings

127   "An amazingly successful American teacher, Marva Collins..."

Read Marva Collins. You don't have to agree with every word she says – I don't – but my goodness is she inspiring!! See Collins, M., & Tamarkin, C. (1982). *Marva Collins' Way*. New York: Penguin Putnam.

135   "...in an excellent book called *The Quiet* by Paul Wilson."

Wilson, P. (2007). *The Quiet*. London: Macmillan.

135   "An obvious genre of stories that indirectly reinforce creativity are creation myths."

A good source for myths generally is Scott Littleton, C. (Ed). (2002). *The Illustrated Anthology of World Myth and Storytelling*. London: Duncan Baird Publishers. You will find others. Older students could exercise their creativity by creating their own myths and stories.

Chapter 10: Thanksgiving, Harvest, Sukkot or Raksha Bandhan

147   "Gratitude is one of the key strengths for enjoying life."

If gratitude is one of your top strengths or one you wish to develop further I would thoroughly recommend the beautiful website **www.gratefulness.org** and a book by a Benedictine monk, David Steindl-Rast, (1984). *Gratefulness, the Heart of Prayer*. Ramsey, NJ: Paulist Press.

150   "A good resource to use would be *Seasons of Thanks*..."

A lovely book of thanks giving prayers and quotes is Tagore, T. (2005). *Seasons of Thanks: Graces and Blessings for Every Home*. New York: Stewart, Tabori & Chang.

Chapter 11: Festivals of Light: Advent, Divali, Hannukah, Eid

168   Individual Strengths Builders for spirituality might include spending time alone..."

The website **www.gratefulness.org** also has links to more information on spirituality in children.

Chapter 12: Performing Arts

181   "The *Atelier* System from Italy..."

A book about the Atelier system is Gandini, L., Cadwell, L., & Schwall, C. (2005). *In the Spirit of the Studio*. London: Teachers College Press.

Chapter 13: Easter: A Celebration of Love, Kindness and Friendship

196   "Kindness, showing care and love towards another person..."

There is a website that is a particularly good source of quotes about kindness called **www.actsofkindness.org**

198   "This strength is based on a combination of intelligences..."

Personal, social and emotional intelligence is one of Peterson and Seligman's 24 character strengths. See Peterson, C. & Seligman, M. E. P. (2004). *Character Strengths and Virtues: A Handbook and Classification*. Oxford: Oxford University Press.

Chapter 14: Our Community

202   "It was there I found the Lincolnshire Tiddy Mun who features in my version..."

Notes on the Tiddy Mun came from Westwood, J., & Simpson, J. (2005). *The Lore of the Land*. London: Penguin Books (p.440)

Chapter 15: Endings

216   "The Forgiveness Project collects stories of extraordinary forgiveness from around the world..."

Stories to inspire you, and for older children to read for themselves, may be found at **www.theforgivenessproject.com**

Chapter 16: Creating Your Own Festivals

228   "They can be faith stories..."

If you are looking for stories on the internet, a good place to start is
http://www.sacred-texts.com/index.htm It has lots of out of copyright
collections of stories – I used it for Beira, Tom Tit Tot, Brendan and
others.

228   *"The Lore of the Land* would help you do this."

Westwood, J., & Simpson, J. (2005). *The Lore of the Land.* London:
Penguin Books.

Appendix:

Sources for Stories Included or Mentioned in the Book

Chapter 9: Beginnings

What is an elephant really like?
By Donelle Blubaugh
Available at: **www.peacecorps.gov**

Chapter 10: Thanksgiving: Harvest, Sukkot, Raksha Bandhan

The Spirit of the Corn
(from the Tuscarora people)
Can be found in Scott Littleton, C. (2002) *The Illustrated Anthology of World Myth and Storytelling*. London: Duncan Baird Publishers.

Chapter 12: Performing Arts

Where is the moon?
The original can be found in:
More English Fairy Tales, by Joseph Jacobs [1894]

The Buried Moon
Can be found at **http://www.sacred-texts.com/neu/eng/meft/index.htm**

Beira Queen of Winter
By Donald Alexander Mackenzie
Can be found at **www.sacred-texts.com**

Chapter 13: Easter: A Celebration of Love, Kindness and Frienship

The Elephant and his Mother
My version is based on one found at:
http://buddhism.kalachakranet.org/resources/buddhist_stories.html

The Story of Guru Nanak
Can be found at **www.sikhnet.com**

The Queen Bee
Can be found at **http://thequeenbee.us/index.html**

A version of the legend of *St. Werburga* can be found at
http://www.britannia.com/bios/saints/werburga.html

Gilgamesh
Can be found in Scott Littleton, C. (2002) *The Illustrated Anthology of World Myth and Storytelling*. London: Duncan Baird Publishers.

Chapter 14: Our Community

The Bremen Town Musicians
A version is retold by Peter Carter in Carter, P. (1982). *Fairy Tales from Grimm*. Oxford: Oxford University Press.

The Magic Paint Brush
This is variously described as a Chinese or an Indian story. The original can be found at **http://www.theserenedragon.net/Tales/china-maling.html** though there are plenty of different versions around.

Chapter 15: Endings

The Selkie Wife
This is quite a famous story. I heard mine from a story teller but there is one in Muir, T. (1998). *The Mermaid Bride and other Orkney Tales*. Kirkwall: Kirkwall Press.

Index

academic year, start of 128
Advent
    see also Christmas
    celebration of 70–1
    and Christian tradition 160
    defined 159
    music associated with 230
    olfactory associations 122
    spirituality 167
    stories associated with 49
    strengths focused on 161
Advent Spiral (moving meditation)
    105, 121
    see also Spiral (walking
        meditation)
age of children, sensitivity to 61
aggressive behaviour, discouraging
    137–8
amygdala, brain 122
anxiety 128, 137
aphorisms 127
Aristotle 22, 154, 221
assemblies
    end of term 131
    endings 216
    festivals 41–2
    'Hopes' 131
    silence in 118
    story telling in 119
    strengths in 117–18
Atelier system 181
auditory learners 105
authenticity 207
autistic children 65, 102
autonomy 102

baking
    of bread 122, 157–8
    and hospitality 146
    and spirituality 167

    Strengths Builder activities 152
Barbour, Lynn 174, 208
beauty, love of 172, 181–2
Beauty and the Beast 196
Beginnings Festival 71, 100, 127,
    128
behaviour, positive habits of 6
*Beira, Queen of Winter (Scottish
    creation myth)* 174, 182
Benno and the Beasts (story) 120
Ben-Shahar, Tal 30, 115
Bettelheim, Bruno 59, 60
bias, side 140
Billy Elliot 182
Billy Goats Gruff, The 173, 177
birthdays 11
Blind Man and the Elephant, The 143
body and mind connections 91–3
body scan meditation 134
Boudicca 203
bravery see courage
bread, baking 122, 157–8
breathing exercises 92
*Brilliant Listening (Strengths Builder
    activity)* 195, 196, 205, 207
*'broaden-and-build' theory of positive
    emotions* 20
Buddhism 192
business, and leadership 205

Caedmon and The First Poem 50, 77
*Cathedral of Our Lady of Chartres,
    The, France* 163
Celebrating Strengths
    see also Strengths Builder
    description and benefits 4
    and festivals 11–12
    see also festivals
    goal 5
    mission statements 116

practising activities and ideas
83
as tool for whole community 43
celebrations
festivals 64–80
music 79
reflection 67–8
training idea 80
Change the Future (Strengths
Builder activity) 219–20
Change the World (Strengths Builder
activity) 148, 151
changes 5, 6, 23, 114, 128
Chanukah *see* Hanukkah festival
character strengths 49, 50
chocolate 27
Chodron, Pema 105
choices 102, 128–9
Choose a Story 175
choral singing 76
Christ Child 171
Christmas
see also Advent
olfactory associations 122
period following 172
run up to, in schools 160
significance of 11, 70
story of 68
Christmas cake 167
Christmas Story 49
church attendance 11
Cinderella 49, 50
citizenship, and teamwork 205–7
Class Gratitude Journal 148
classroom
curiosity, development of 137
environment 97–8, 116
flow in 29, 101–3
happiness, importance of 23
story telling in 109
strengths in 98–9
Strengths Builders 99–100
teamwork 180
clear thinking 142
coaching, Strengths Builders based
on 13, 41, 43
Collins, Marva 127
colour 230
Colour Box (Strengths Builder
activity) 74, 106–7
comfort zones 29

community 201–12
and festivals 231
global 203
national 202
regional 202
school councils 206
teamwork and citizenship
205–7
compliments 198–9
compliments chair 199
container, concept 57
cooking 146, 167
co-operative groups 206
courage 174–7
Courage Meditation 40–1, 104
defined 174
encouragement of group 176
endurance 175
and learning 174
public speaking 175
self esteem, building 30
stretch zones 29
Create a Story Space (Strengths
Builder activity)
authenticity 207
beauty, love of 182–6
hope and optimism 163
meditative activities 29
moving meditations 106
objectives 7–8
persistence 178
prudence 222
reflection 74
self control 219
creation myths 135–6, 174, 182
creativity 132–6
Csikszentmihalyi, Mihaly 27
curiosity 137–8
curriculum 5, 7–8, 55–6, 132
customer service training, use of
WOW activity 142
customs, reassuring nature of 129

dance 77
Datkiewicz, Tony 19
death 191
deficit model, education based on
34
displays 16, 89, 116
Divali festival 161
Drake, Francis 203

dyslexia 36

Easter 190–200
    and kindness 72, 116
    and meditation 74
    music associated with 230
    olfactory associations 78
    and resurrection 191, 192
eating, emotional reasons 214–15
Ector, Sir 209, 210
education
    deficit model, based on 36
    positive psychology in 19–33
    strengths in 38–40
Eeyore Thoughts (Strengths Builder
        activity)
    body and mind connections 95
    and explanatory style 95
    forgiveness 217–18
    hope and optimism 163
    optimistic thinking 44
    persistence 178
    positive habits 26
    self control 220
    suggestions for 96
    tolerance 142
effort, praising 86–7, 138–9, 178
Eid, festival of 161
elephants 143–4
Elephant and His Mother, The
        (Buddhist story) 50, 72,
        196, 199–200
Elizabeth I 203
emotional intelligence ix, x, 198
emotional literacy 9, 17, 57
emotional maturity 9
Emotional Experience of Learning and
        Teaching, The 65
emotions
    after taste, emotional 90
    controlling 42
    emotional eating 214–15
    endings 213, 214
    hope and optimism 162–6
    managing 89–91
    positive 104, 193
        see also Strengths; Strengths
            Builders
    stories as medium for 56–7
    television, effect on 90

uncomfortable 89
empathy 217
Encouragement (Strengths Builder
    activity) 176
endings 212–25
    assemblies 216
    concept 71
    emotions evoked by 213, 214
    school day/school year 212–13
    year in school, final 214
Endings Festival 71, 214
endorphins 76
endurance 175
enjoyment 23, 232
environment
    auditory 123
    of classroom 116
    emotional 116–17
    learning 139
    physical 8, 14
Excellent Listening 135
explanatory style 93–6
external motivation 138

'factual' questions 110
failures
    inner cities, children from 22
    memories of 25
    perception of 30, 180
    reframing 24
fairness 153–6
fairy tales 60
    see also specific fairy tales, such as
        Billy Goats Gruff
families, observation of 66–7
Feast of Tabernacles (Sukkot) 145
feasts 214–15
Feelings Rain (Strengths Builder
        activity) 154, 155
Feelings Story Scroll 219
festivals 11–12
    see also Beginnings Festival;
        Hanukkah festival; harvest
        festivals; Raksha Bandhan
        (thanksgiving festival);
        Sukkot (Feast of
        Tabernacles)
    annual 37
    assemblies 41–2
    Beginnings 100

celebration of 67–8
and celebrations 64–80
and colours 128
creating one's own 226–32
cycles of 66–7, 70
    rhythm created by 121
Endings 214
and food 78, 129, 229–30
ingredients 228–32
of light 159–61
and mental health 64–6
and music 128
Muslim faith 227
non-Christian 72–3
and reflection 228
resilience skills 42–3
seasonality 69–70, 78
and singing 77
and stories 74–5
and strengths 37, 42–3, 51, 75–6,
    228
traditional 15
at whole school level 16, 120–1
Finding Nemo (film) 180
flourishing 21, 83
flow (optimal functioning) 25–7
    in classroom 101–3
    small choices, introducing 102
    very young children 28
flowers, and sense memories 123
focusing 22, 37
food
    'comfort' 214
    and festivals 78, 129, 229–30
    sense memories 123
forgiveness 37, 215, 216–18
Forgiveness Project 216, 218
Four Musicians, The 207
fractals, and nature 79
Fredrickson, B. L. 20
Friends Reunited (website) 3
friendship 197–9
Funny Stories 169

generosity 150–3
Gingerbread Man, The 136
goal setting 130, 163
Goals assembly 131
God/Creator 135
Godly play (Montessori RE

method) 61–2
Goldilocks 156
Goleman, Daniel ix
Good Bits/Bad Bits (Strengths
    Builder activity) 141, 196,
    217
good news, response to 195
Goodbye Mog 49
Grace 150
gratitude 147–50
group identity 206
groups, strengths of 40
Guru Nanak, story of 192

habits, positive see positive habits
Hansel and Gretel 49
Hanukkah festival 72–3, 161
hao-xue-xin see love of learning
happiness, importance of 20–1
    happy memories 23–6, 122, 131
Harold, King 203
harvest festivals 69, 71, 78
hippocampus, brain 122
honesty 207, 208
hope 31–2, 162–6
hospitality 146–7
Hospitality (Strengths Builder
activity) 121
'hot' intelligences 198
How Do I Feel? (Strengths Builder
    activity) 196, 198, 219
humour 161, 168, 169

Ignatian prayer 108
integrity 207, 208
intelligences, and friendship 198
Invitations (Strengths Builder
activity) 152
Isaiah 169–70

Jamie's School Dinners 152
Jesus, death of 191, 192
Joke Book Competition 169
jokes 168, 169
Judeo-Christian-Islamic myths 135
justice 153

Kay, Sir 209, 210
kinaesthetic learners 105
kindness 72, 116, 196–7

The Kindness Catcher 197

labelling of children 178–81
labyrinth walking (prayer form)
    163
LAUGHS acronym 155, 219
laughter 137–8, 168
Lazy Jack 169
leadership 38, 204–5
learning, love of 136–40
Levy, Amanda 142
life satisfaction 41
Linley, Alex 87
Lipman, Mathew 109
Lipschutz, Israel 203
Listen to Your Breath Meditation
    105, 134, 151
listening training 176
Little Red Riding Hood 52, 222
Little Match Girl, The 59
Little Red Hen, The 156
Looking or Listening Walk 106
Lore of the Land, The 202, 228
love 193–6
love of learning 5, 39–40

Magic Brush, The 56, 59
Magic Paintbrush, The 59, 207
Malaga 66
mantras 104, 105
Mary and Joseph 170
meditation 103–5
    benefits 104
    bread making as 146
    calming meditations 107–8
    creativity 134
    and flow 29
    Meditation (Strengths Builder
        activity) 142, 178, 219, 228
    moving meditations 105
    as Strengths Builder 104
    Tree Meditation 208
    visual 108
    visualisation 107
    walking 163–5
memories
    failures and bad events 25
    good 108
    happy 23–6, 131
    of relatives 3–4

sense 122, 123
smell, sense of 78–9
and smell, sense of 230
mental health, and festivals 64–6
metaphors 49
Misereri (Allegri) 230
mission statements 116
mocking laughter, discouraging
    137–8
modelling 8–9, 176, 217
modesty 88
Mollie Whuppie 136
Mood Boosters (Strengths Builder
        activity)
    as class level Strengths Builders
        15
    classroom activities 111, 112
    creativity 132
    fairness 155
    friendship 198
    generosity 151
    persistence 178
    personal, building 90
    tolerance 142
    training idea 113
moral judgement 153
motivation, extrinsic and intrinsic
    138
Musicians of Bremen, The 207
music 79, 123, 128, 230–1
Muslim faith 227

nation, celebrating 202
negative bias 90
Nelson 202
Nightingale, Florence 203

Oliver, Jamie 152
open ended activities 129
open mindedness 140, 141, 142,
    143
open questions, use of 195–6
Opinion Lines (Strengths Builder
    activity) 133, 175, 217
optimism 31–2, 60, 93, 94, 95,
    162–6
Other Uses (game) 135

panic zones 30
patience 88

Pearls (Strengths Builder activity)
    as end of term assembly 131
    endings 216
    and festivals 228
    generosity 151
    gratitude 148
    happy memories, recalling 24
    hope and optimism 33, 163
    positive endings 112–13
    preparation for learning 26, 27
    prudence 222
    reflection 73
    spirituality 167
    as visualisation 108
Peerie Fool 61, 136
Pentecost, feast of 211
perceptions, changing 36–8
Performing Arts Festival 72, 77,
    172–89
persistence 86, 178
personal intelligence 198
personal leadership 205
pessimism 93–4
Peterson, Chris 35
    on character strengths and
        virtues 49
    on cognitive strengths 131
    on flow 28
    list of strengths 10, 35, 88
    on love of learning and
        curiosity 137
    terminology 76
    on 'transcendent' strengths *see*
        'transcendent' strengths
Philosophy (Strengths Builder
        activity)
    authenticity 207
    and building of strengths 88
    courage 175
    creativity 133
    fairness 154, 155
    forgiveness 217
    gratitude 149
    love 196
    love of learning 138
philosophy, use in classroom
    109–11
Philosophy with Children 140
physical environment 8, 14
Pied Piper 60

playfulness 169
positive habits
    building 20–2, 41, 59–60
    forming 6
    happy memories, fostering of
        24, 26
positive psychology
    and Aristotle 22
    in education 19–33
    ethos of school 16
    habits 22
    origin and role ix
    Seligman on 19–20
    Strengths Builders taken from
        41
Positive Workplace Alliance 13
praise, importance of 31, 86–7, 87,
    178
preparation for learning 26–7, 58,
    103
pretend play 129
priming 85, 115
    of environment 8, 14
props, use of 106
prudence 215, 221–2
public speaking 175

Queen Bee, The 51, 75, 196–7
questions, 'thinking' and 'factual'
    110
Quiet, The (Wilson) 134

Rain Stick Listening (moving
        meditation) 29, 74, 105,
        134, 135
Rain Stick Meditation 151
Rain Stick Walking (moving
        meditation) 134
Raksha Bandhan (thanksgiving
        festival) 73, 145
reflection 160
    and celebration 67–8
    and festivals 228
    and gratitude 148
    and Strengths Builders 73–4
    suggestions for 80
Reflections (Strengths Builder
        activity) 73, 151, 154, 208,
        222, 228
region, celebrating 202

rejoicing, act of 146
relationships 153, 193, 194
religious practice 166
resilience 32, 42–3
responsibility 206
resurrection 192
ridiculous, sense of 169
Road to Bethlehem, The (Strengths Builder activity) 119, 160, 167, 169–71, 191
Road to Jerusalem, The (Strengths Builder activity) 74, 119, 191, 196
Rumpelstiltskin 61, 136, 156, 220, 222

Same/Different 141
Save the World (Strengths Builder activity) 206
Savouring 108, 151, 220
school councils 206
Scottish creation myths 136, 174, 182
seasonality, festivals 69–70, 78
Seasons of Thanks: Graces and Blessings for Every Home 150
self awareness 207, 219
self control 218–20
self esteem 30, 31, 86, 174–5
self-awareness 160
Seligman, Martin 35
    on character strengths and virtues 49
    on cognitive strengths 131
    on happiness 21
    list of strengths 10, 35, 88
    on love of learning and curiosity 137
    on memories 24–5
    on optimistic thinking 32
    on positive psychology ix, 19–20
    terminology 76
    on 'transcendent' strengths see 'transcendent' strengths
Selkie Wife, The 215, 218, 223–5
sensitivity 194
sensory impressions, in school 122–3
setbacks 25, 44
Shepherds, The 170–1

Sign Language 120
silence, in assemblies 118
Silent Thank You 149
singing, and strengths 76–7
skills, resilience 42–3
slumping, effect of 91–2
SMART acronym 163
smell, sense of 78–9, 122, 230
smiling 108
Snow White 48
social intelligence 198, 199
Society for Storytelling, National Storytelling Week (UK) 71, 173
Speakers and Listeners (Strengths Builder activity) 176, 195, 205, 207
special needs, children with 65, 102
speech, positive habits of 6
Spiral (walking meditation) 74, 163–5, 166
Spirit of the Corn (Native American Indian story) 120, 150, 156–7
spirituality 166, 166–8
St. Columba, story of 218
St. Werburga, story of 120, 197
stationery boxes, use in meditation 106–7
stories 11, 46–63, 228–9
    age of children, sensitivity to 61
    celebration of 229
    and character strengths 50
    fairy tales 60
    and festivals 74–5
    mood, boosting 58–9
    negative 25–6
    positive thought habits, building 59–60
    as preparation for learning 58
    as repair medium 58
    sacred 57
    sad 60–1
    and strengths 49–52
    strengths, linking with curriculum 55–6
    as teaching tool 12, 47–9
    traditional 12, 41, 47, 55, 75, 173, 193

values and emotions, medium
    for 56–7
  writing 55
'Story Chest' 106
Story Scroll 155
story telling
  see also Story Telling (Strengths
    Builder activity)
  benefits for children 54
  calming nature of 26
  in classroom 109
  joke telling distinguished 169
  long-term influence 46–7
  oral 52
  as powerful tool 52–4
  props, use of 106
  reading a story distinguished
    12, 53, 119
  tolerance, encouraging 141
  training idea 63
  types of 61–2
  at whole school level 118–20
Story Telling Meditations 108
Story Telling (Strengths Builder
    activity)
  authenticity 207
  and building of strengths 88
  courage 175
  creativity 133
  fairness 155
  gratitude 149
  hope and optimism 163
  objectives 7–8
  persistence 180
  prudence 222
  at whole school level 121
strengths
  see also Celebrating Strengths;
    Strengths Builders
  in assemblies 117–18
  building 21, 88–9
  in classroom 98–9
  cognitive 131
  defined 34–6
  displaying 89
  in education 38–40
  and festivals 37, 40–1, 51, 75–6,
    228
  of groups 40
  list of 8, 35

  see also 'transcendent'
    strengths
  listening for 86–7
  qualities 10
  and resilience 42–3
  and singing 76–7
  and stories 49–52
  top 36, 37, 38
    teachers 100–1
  VIA Classification 35, 84
  in wider school 115–17
Strengths Builders
  see also Celebrating Strengths;
    specific Strengths Builders;
    strengths
  adult coaching tools, based
    upon 13, 41, 43
      and building of strengths
        88
  'child friendly' 43
  children conducting their own
    150, 166
  at class level 14–15, 231
  and classroom 99–100
  courage 178
  defined 13
  getting started 17
  individual ideas 140
  at individual level 13–14, 231
  meditation 104
      see also meditation
  positive psychology, taken from
    41
  and reflection 73–4
  for spirituality 168
  use by teachers 41
  at whole school level 15–16,
    114–23, 231
Strengths Gym 40–1, 41, 88, 99,
    100
Strengths Spotting (Strengths
    Builder activity) 51, 179,
    181, 199, 206–7
stretch zones 28, 29–30
structure 128, 130
success, meaning 30–1
Sukkot (Feast of Tabernacles) 145
Sword in the Stone 208–11
synonyms 115

Take the Lead (Strengths Builder activity) 99–100
tales *see* stories
tea making, as calming meditation 107
teachers
    enthusiasm and humour strengths 39
    goal setting 130
    humour, use of 168
    long-term influence 3, 4
    love of learning 39–40, 139
    pupils, love of 194
    Strengths Builders, use of 41, 44, 84
    top strengths 100–1
teaching 8, 12, 40, 132
teamwork 180, 203, 205–7
television, effect on emotions 90
Ten Lepers, The 150
Thank You Letters 150
thankfulness 145, 146
Thanksgiving 145
'thinking questions' 110
thought, positive habits of 6
thought control 217–18
Three Feathers, The 140
Three Little Pigs, The 51, 140
Tiddy Mun 188, 202
tolerance 140–3
    of ourselves 142
Tom Tit Tot 136
traditional stories 60–1
traits 20
'transcendent' strengths
    beauty, love of 181
    defined 182
    fairness 153–6
    gratitude 147
    humour 161, 168
Treasure Chest (Strengths Builder activity) 91, 123
    classroom activities 111–12
    fairness 155
    generosity 151

hope and optimism 32
persistence 178, 181
personal, building 91
training idea 123
Tree Meditation 208

values 34–5, 56–7
VIA Classification of Strengths 35, 84
virtues 20
visualisation 107

weaknesses 21, 36–7
What a Mess 58
What Went Well (WWW) 18
    body and mind connections 95
    and explanatory style 95
    generosity 151
    gratitude 148
    hope and optimism 163
    love of learning 140
    persistence 178
    prudence 222
    reflection 73
    self control 220
    spirituality 167
What's New? (classroom activity) 139
Where is the Moon? 180, 186–9, 202
Where There's a Will (Strengths Builder activity) 162, 181, 220, 222, 224
Wilson, Paul 134
wisdom 88
Wise Men, The 171
Wishing Others Well (WOW) 142–3, 143, 217
Word Meditation 104

Young Leaders Award 205

Zen and the Art of Relaxation 230–1
zone 102

Printed in the United States
114483LV00001B/22/A